GETTING THERE FROM HERE

GETTING THERE FROM HERE

MEDITATIONS FOR
THE JOURNEY

DAVID OWEN

St. Mark's United Methodist Church
Bloomington, Indiana

Getting There from Here: Meditations for the Journey
was published by St. Mark's United Methodist Church,
Bloomington, Indiana. Proceeds from this printing will
go for St. Mark's mission outreach projects.

Design and composition by CompuType, Bloomington.
Cover and title page art by David Owen.

Printed in the United States of America

Library of Congress Catalog Card Number: 95-071890

ISBN 1-878318-49-7

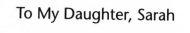

To My Daughter, Sarah

CONTENTS

Introduction · *ix*

While It Is Still Dark, A Bird Is Singing · 1

If We Have Lost Our Heart · 7

Foregrounds and Backgrounds · 13

Blind Spots · 20

The All-You-Can-Eat Colander Diet · 25

The High Cost of Knuckling Under · 32

Roots, Vines, and Branches · 40

Laying Hold of God · 47

Elephants in Our Living Room · 52

Thank God It's Summer · 59

When Life Presents Us with Hills · 66

Ghosts · 72

All Things Are Possible · 77

O For a Thousand Ears to Hear · 85

Had Jesus Lived a Hundred Years · 91

The Gift of Encouragement · 98

Is the Sound of Truth One Octave Too High? · 105

Disturbing the Peace · 111

When Wounds Are Transformed · 118

Restoration · 123

Treasure Worth Having · 130

Drainage Ditches for Jesus · 136

Don't Let Your Death Stop You · 143

. . . Forever. Amen · 149

· INTRODUCTION ·

THE ANCIENT CHINESE philosophy of Taoism teaches that there is a Way in life—a natural path of nonviolence which meanders through life's open doors and empty spaces. Water winding its way through tiny openings as it trickles down a hill is a familiar example of this. This ancient image has long appealed to me, and I find it personally helpful to assume that no matter where I am there is a way to move forward in life. Then the task is not to wonder whether there is a way, but to discover and travel it. Here, in my mind's eye, I see Moses and the Hebrew people standing on the banks of the Red Sea with Pharaoh's troops hotly pursuing them. It would appear that all is lost. But, wait! There is a path to freedom immediately before them, as Moses discovers when he puts his foot in the sea. Jesus, too, speaks of an ever-present Way that leads toward life and urges that we enter by the narrow gate—which I take to mean the God-given path of possibility which always exists. That narrow gate may require us to squeeze or stretch. If we are hanging onto our baggage like camels, we may not be able to pass through until we surrender our humps. Still, there is a Way. Even in death an opening is created, when the stone sealing us off from life is rolled away.

This basic teaching is a comfort and inspiration to me. When I wander from the path, or the path that I am treading proves to be a dead end, or a bridge that I have been counting on is washed away, I remind myself that if it is Life that we are after, we can always get there from here. The Kingdom, Jesus said, is at hand. Like Paul, I do not boast that I have attained this prize, but have long believed that Life is the only prize worth seeking. The sermons that follow, which were preached at St. Mark's United Methodist Church in Bloomington, Indiana, during 1990–1995, are born of observations made along the way.

I am grateful for the many persons who assisted and encouraged this effort and especially thank Bruce Carpenter of Computype who proposed this book and himself designed and prepared it for printing. Thanks to Bruce's generous gift of time and talent, all proceeds earned by this edition will be used to extend the mission outreach of St. Mark's United Methodist Church.

While It Is Still Dark, A Bird Is Singing

❖   ❖   ❖

Even as you appeared to Moses, because
I need you, you appear to me, not
often, however. I live essentially
in darkness. You are perhaps training me to be
responsive to the slightest brightening.

— Louise Glück (in *The Wild Iris*)

I F YOU TYPICALLY rise before the sun—especially in spring and summer—you know that there is always at least one bird that starts singing before the dawn. If you notice the singing and lift your head to observe the sunrise, you will see only darkness instead. Indeed, some prophets, song writers and naturalists say that the darkness deepens just before the dawn. If asked, the bird that is singing in advance of the sun might tell you that she sings because she knows that the sun is coming. Actually, she doesn't know. She trusts. When it is still dark, no one knows for certain that the sun is coming. If ever you sat up all night rocking a feverish child or listening to an asthmatic parent fight for breath, then you know how deep the darkness can be and how long the night actually is. That is why it is such a comfort to hear the song of the first bird. When the first bird is singing, something primordial within us begins to trust.

II

GEORGE BUTTRICK was a prominent preacher in America when I was in college and for one semester he was my preaching professor at Garrett Theological Seminary in Evanston, Illinois.

In one of his sermons George Buttrick said something like this: "Some people say that life is all growth and others say that it is all decay, when, in truth, life is both decay and growth, both growth and decay."

We could make the same statement about light and darkness. Some people say that life is all light and others say that it is all darkness, when, in truth, life is both darkness and light, both light and darkness. If we do not see any light, we are not paying attention. We are in active denial if we do not see any darkness.

In its more radiant forms, Christianity may deny that there is any darkness. I have heard religiously fervent people say, "Since I met Jesus I have only known joy, love, light and peace—Jesus took away all my darkness." Some radiant New Agers have a similar perception: "There is no tragedy or evil," I have heard some say. "All is light; everything that happens is chosen by us or is divinely intended." By contrast, Christianity in its more orthodox forms has always known that there is darkness in life. Each year the four weeks of Advent are intended to remind us of the darkness—not only the darkness outside in places like Bosnia or Rwanda, but also the darkness inside—inside our own country, our own cities, our own lives and our own hearts. In part, Advent is a call to notice and face the darkness—both the darkness outside and the darkness within. If we say there is no darkness, we are deceiving ourselves and the truth is not in us.

III

When I was a child between the ages of two and ten, I spent much of my time as a patient in hospitals. Visiting hours were more strict back then. I remember one long hospitalization that seemed particularly lonely. I'm guessing that I was eight. For several weeks I was in a large ward of cribs and children's beds—there must have been ten children in the ward but I can't recall many interactions. The ward was only half full and there was an empty bed between each of us. The visiting hours were longer on Sundays, but on weekdays they began exactly at one o'clock and were over at two. I could tell it was my mother when I heard her heels clicking down the hall at 1:01. I also listened to her fading footsteps when she left at two. It was winter in Milwaukee, then, which meant that it was dark by five o'clock in the afternoon and stayed dark until eight in the morning. The winter nights were long. My mother brought me a flashlight and for a while I passed some of the time at night by reading surreptitiously under the blankets. The flashlight and the books helped me to cope with the darkness. One night, a nurse saw a suspicious glow, whipped back the covers, and took away the book and my flashlight. The book was titled *Old Hickory* and was about President Andrew Jackson. The nights were longer after that. I always awoke hours before daybreak and waited for the hospital's day to begin.

Several mornings a week something wonderful happened. My bed was beside a window, overlooking the alley. Even though it was still dark, I could tell that the morning was coming as soon as I heard the clop, clop, clop, clop of the milkman's horse and the creak of his wagon. If I strained to look out the window I could see his shadow beneath the street light. Then sounds of the horse stopped and were replaced by the rattle of milk bottles, as the milkman made his delivery.

Hallelujah! I'd made it! The clop, clop, clop, clop of the milkman's horse was my first bird. Morning, breakfast, sunlight, people, nurses were all at hand. As my favorite theologian, Paul Tillich, might have said, "Nothing had changed." But the instant I heard the clop, clop, clop, clop of the milkman's horse, "Everything was transformed."

To say that Jesus saves us from the darkness—which he can—is not to say that he makes all the darkness go away. He doesn't. Everyone with the courage to look knows that in the world much darkness remains. But for those who trust, Jesus is the song of the first bird. To say that Jesus is the Good News doesn't mean that you and I will never know darkness again, but that for those who are trying to hang on until the dawn, he is the clatter of the milkman's horse and the creak of the wagon. For people with eyes to see, Jesus represents a slight brightening that foretells the dawn.

IV

It's interesting to me that in the Northern Hemisphere, at least, we celebrate Christmas at the darkest time of the year. You might say, "Why, of course we do—December 25th is Christ's birthday!" But the Church has never known the exact day on which Jesus was born. Indeed, we're not entirely clear on the year. The scholarly consensus these days is that Jesus was born in the year 4 A.D. But we never knew the exact day. Wanting to celebrate the birth of Jesus, the Roman Church just picked a day. They came very close to picking the darkest day, dropping Christmas into the Roman world's celebration of the Winter Solstice. I assume that they intended that. That tells us a little something about what faith is. The Church boldly selects the darkest season to announce that the light is coming. The Church picks the coldest season of the year to tell us that warmth is near.

When John the Baptist, who is also associated with the Season of Advent in Christian tradition, saw the darkness of his time, he made a gut-level call about what was coming. Violence, injustice and corruption were rampant and, seeing them, John decided that Judgment was coming. Destruction was coming. "Even now God's ax is measuring the root of the tree," John said. John saw God as getting ready to slap human history aside the head. Like those "Prepare to Meet Your God" signs you used to see on country highways, John was warning people to clean up their act before the coming of a harsh Judge.

Looking at the very same darkness, Jesus made a different call. Instead of saying that Judgment and Destruction were coming, Jesus said that Light and Love were coming. Jesus said that the Kingdom of God was coming. Indeed, the Kingdom of God was at hand. That was his way of saying that despite the darkness, hopeful possibilities were present. Is what we see what we get?

V

ON THANKSGIVING EVE some of you attended the joint worship service in which St. Mark's participated again this year. We have seven congregations participating now. The Unitarian-Universalists who hosted the service, Congregation Beth Shalom, and five Christian congregations. Rev. Gregory Wilson of the Bethel African Methodist Episcopal Church was the preacher that night. As he began his sermon, Rev. Wilson asked everybody to stand up and then said, "I must be me! I can't preach to you tonight without being me!" Then he asked each person to find someone he or she didn't know. "Now join hands with this stranger," the Rev. Mr. Wilson said. "Look them in the eye and say aloud, 'I love you!'" After we had done that, he told us to add, "And there's nothing you can do about it!"

I liked that: "Stranger, I love you and there is nothing you can do about it." That reminded me that Christian love is not a feeling. Christian love is a decision. Christian love is an attitude—a way of approaching another person or life. Christian love is an angle of attack. It looks people in the eye and says, "I love you . . . and there is nothing you can do about it."

VI

CHRISTIAN HOPE is also like that. Christian hope—or, if you prefer, Christmas hope—is a decision, not a feeling. Christian hope believes in daybreak, but not because all the pain, tragedy, loneliness, death and darkness have gone. Anyone can believe in daybreak after all the pain, tragedy, loneliness, death and darkness have gone. Christian hope believes that daybreak is coming despite the darkness. Christian hope believes that daybreak is coming because of the brightening that was glimpsed in Jesus Christ. Christian hope believes in daybreak because, even though it is still dark, one bird is already singing. Christian hope believes that dawn is near because it hears the clatter of the milkman's horse and the creak of his wagon. Soon the wagon will stop and the bottles will begin rattling. Christian hope looks the world's darkness straight in the eye and says, "I'm going to live as though the light is coming—I'm going to live as though God is coming—I'm going to live as though joy and peace and love and justice are coming . . . and there is nothing you can do about it!" Christian hope trains its heart to be cheered by the lighting of a single candle. Christian hope trains its heart to be responsive to even the slightest brightening.

December 1994

If We Have Lost Our Heart

◆   ◆   ◆

Where is my heart gone?
> — Henry David Thoreau

AN ADVENT SCRIPTURE passage from the Hebrew prophet Zephaniah says:

> Rejoice and exult with all your heart,
> O daughter of Jerusalem.
> [For] The King of Israel, the Lord,
> is in your midst.

But what if we no longer have a song in our heart? I do not intend this merely as a Christmas question, but as a life question: What can we do, if there is no longer a song in our heart?

II

IN JANUARY 1842 John Thoreau, the brother whom Henry David Thoreau loved especially, was struck down by an unusual fever. In only three days he died. Two and a half months later, Henry David Thoreau, still deeply mourning the death of his brother, asked himself this poignant question in his morning journal:

> Where is my heart gone? They say men cannot part with it and live.

Nor can we live. We can exist, but we cannot live—if our heart is gone.

Do you know the emptiness of which Thoreau was speaking? Has there been any season of your life in which your heart was gone? Did you find it hard to live when your heart was gone?

Losing our heart is a serious matter. Far more serious than simply feeling sad. When our heart is gone we lose more than happiness. When our heart is gone we also lose our faith—we may think of that as losing our faith in God, but we also lose our faith in life. When our heart is gone we cannot find our reason for living—we lose our ability to make sense of life. When our heart is gone we lose our courage to face life and our ability to trust life. We can exist but we cannot live when our heart is gone. It is as though we were dead when our heart is gone. What can we do when our heart is gone?

III

I CAN ADMIT to you that there have been seasons in my life during which I knew that I had lost my heart. Once, because of that, I left the pastoral ministry for three years. It is very difficult to be a faithful minister of Jesus Christ when your heart is gone.

In my experience there are two ways for human beings to lose their heart. One way is not to pay attention to your heart— to ignore the promptings of your heart or to betray the deepest desires of your heart, and to do so over a long period of time. Losing our heart doesn't happen overnight. But one day we will find that we have lost our heart, if for too long a time we have paid no attention to our heart.

Paying attention to our heart is not as easy as it sounds. It does not merely mean paying attention to our momentary desires. What makes it so difficult to be human is that when we are human, momentary desires which tomorrow will mean nothing to us at all can today masquerade as the deepest longings of our heart. One reason that I worship—one reason that I pray—is that I have learned from experience that it is in God's Presence and God's Presence alone that I have half a chance of knowing the difference between my momentary desires and the deepest longings of my heart. Even in God's presence that kind of sorting can be difficult work. The Bible says that when Jesus was doing that kind of sorting in the Garden of Gethsemane on the night before his death, it was such difficult, agonizing work that he found himself sweating great drops of blood. If it was hard work for Jesus, I don't expect that it will be easy work for me. But there is perhaps no work more important than this, that we bow down before God with as much openness and honesty as we can, asking God's help in sorting out the difference between our momentary desires and the deepest longings of our heart. If we have lost heart, we will not gain heart, until we pay serious attention to the deepest longings of our heart. Doing our best to listen at that level is difficult business. That is why the Bible depicts people as praying earnestly, and praying while in agony, and praying from out of the depths.

The second way to lose our heart is to not pay attention to life—to refuse to notice and acknowledge the true nature of life, until life in its rawness, power, and mystery crashes in and overturns us. I read recently of a ninety-three-year-old woman who lost her heart when she learned that she was dying. She had not been paying attention to life. The possibility of her own death seemed unfair to her and she asked, "Why me?" I am not wanting to be unsympathetic. Nevertheless, if what is keeping us going is that we have hidden from the true nature of life, then one day life may reveal itself in such an unexpectedly shocking way as to cause us to lose our faith, our courage, our meaning, and our trust. If we do not pay attention to the nature of life, we are in danger of losing our heart.

IV

ONE OF MY FAVORITE Bible stories is about two men who had lost heart. They lost heart when Jesus whom they had followed was killed. They were walking on the road from Jerusalem to Emmaus on the third day after Jesus' execution. Each was asking the question that Henry David Thoreau asked after his brother unexpectedly died:

> Where is my heart gone? They say men cannot part with it and live.

The disciples walking on the Emmaus Road were despondent because they had never considered the possibility that Jesus would die. Their failure to consider this possibility showed that they had not been paying attention to Jesus, and they certainly had not been paying attention to life. Therefore, when Jesus died, all the meaning went out of their lives. They believed that Jesus had deceived them or that God had betrayed them by allowing Jesus to die. That they did not expect Jesus to die shows that they were not paying attention to life.

Interestingly, the despairing followers of Jesus regained their hearts—they felt their hearts again burning within them— when a stranger met them as they walked along the road and explained to them that Jesus' death was in accordance with the Scriptures. Jesus was not disqualified as the Messiah because he had been killed. Nor had God betrayed them. If they had paid attention to the Scriptures and to life, they would have known that even the Messiah must die. The despondent disciples regained their hearts, by believing that God was present in life as it actually was—not in life as they had merely wished it would be or had expected that it would be. If we do not find God in our life as it actually is, we are in danger of losing our heart.

In the Christmas story from Matthew, Joseph the carpenter from Nazareth was himself in danger of losing his heart. The Bible tells us almost nothing about Mary and Joseph or about whatever love was between them. Given their times, we assume that the marriage between them was arranged and that theirs was not what we think of as a romantic love. Tradition further suggests that Mary was a young woman, perhaps as young as fifteen years old, and that Joseph (some traditions say that he was a widower) was an older man. Yet knowing what human beings are, is it not reasonable to expect that Joseph's heart had been made lighter and happier because of Mary and that he was looking forward to their wedding? Then word came to Joseph that Mary, his betrothed, was with child. That was not what Joseph expected—that was not what Joseph wanted. Can we not assume that Joseph was emotionally injured? Because of his hurt, Joseph decided to quietly end his relationship with Mary. Joseph decided to walk away. This shows us that Joseph was in danger of losing his heart.

How did Joseph regain his heart? Joseph had a dream. Joseph did not have an illusion—Joseph did not pretend that Mary was without child—he did not try to believe that life was the way he wanted it. Instead, Joseph had a dream. What he decided, on the basis of his dream, was that Mary's unexpected child was a part of God's plan for them. Joseph decided to accept the child as Mary's child, as his own child and as God's Child. Joseph chose to love his life situation as it actually was—to find God in his situation as it actually was—and little by little that allowed him to regain his heart.

V

MAY SARTON IS a poet and novelist who is in her early eighties. I have read some of her journals and I see in her a woman who has been in frequent danger of losing her heart. In her sixty-fifth year, May Sarton was trying to recover from two bitter blows that had occurred earlier in the year. Then, in addition, her body was invaded by cancer and a breast was removed surgically. Throughout the year she tried and tried to manufacture a new heart, but no matter how hard she tried, still she felt abandoned and devalued at the center of her being. Late in the year she said that she had learned this:

> It is becoming clear to me that just as poems cannot be written on will, so also recovery from the blows of last November cannot be achieved by will. My own efforts have come to a dead end.

Apparently the human heart comes without bootstraps. The way that May Sarton regained her heart is unexpected and interesting. Rather than continuing to cling to a love relationship that she very much wanted to be permanent, she decided to let go of the relationship, to admit that it was not working and to accept the fact that she was living alone and would be living alone as far into the future as she could see. Within a matter of weeks her life began to change. Her entry for Friday, October 12th, of that year was published in her book, *Recovering: A Journal*—

> What has changed in a miraculous way is the landscape of my heart, so somber and tormented for over a year that I was not myself. Did letting go last month do it? Quite suddenly some weeks ago my inner landscape became luminous and peaceful, no anger, no irritation. . . . The fog has lifted. Whatever the cause, it feels like a miracle.

VI

IF WE HAVE lost our heart, how can we regain it? Might we regain our heart the way May Sarton did inside her house in Maine, the way the disciples did on the Emmaus Road and the way Joseph did following his dream—that is, by considering the possibility that whatever our life looks like externally, God is nevertheless within our life right now? Is it possible that life as we actually have it is an expression of God's love for us?

I believe that our first task is to face our lives honestly. Our second task is to pray that God will speak to us in the deepest stirrings of our heart. It is my experience that even when life is not as we want it—perhaps especially when life is not as we want it—God will speak to us in the unexpected stirrings of our heart. When we listen to God inside, despite whatever is going on outside, we increase the chances that we will again find our heart.

December 1994

Foregrounds and Backgrounds

◆　◆　◆

Jesus stood still and said, "Call him here."

— Mark 10:49

ON WHAT DO YOU focus in life? What do you almost always notice? By contrast, what do you rarely experience or see? Human beings, far more than any other known animals, can adjust their sensory systems. We can tune in or tune out; we can heighten or depress our feelings; we can scan the horizon with our telescopic lens, move in for a close-up or go into a trance-like soft focus. Despite this flexibility, the human brain has certain built-in biases. For example, when we are not thinking about it, our brain will always notice the foreground rather than the background. We miss a lot of reality because of this.

II

WHEN I GO to the movies, most of the time I am looking just where the director wants me to look—he is deciding for me where the action is. But every now and then I like to re-focus on the background. Sometimes there are lots of interesting things going on in the background. So interesting sometimes, that I wonder if they are there by accident or whether the director very carefully included them. Alfred Hitchcock movies were fun in that regard. Hitchcock was the director but he always appeared in one scene in his movies, almost daring the viewer to find him. For those of you who are too young to remember Alfred Hitchcock films, trying to find him while watching one of his mysteries was a primitive form of "Where's

Waldo?" Only rarely did I recognize Hitchcock the first time I viewed one of his films, because I was usually focused on the central action and he was off to the side somewhere—standing at a bus stop, perhaps, or walking through a revolving door. Hitchcock was hard to find because we naturally focus on the foreground and he hid around the edges or in the background. Often it requires intentionality—it requires the use of our higher powers—if we are to look beyond the foreground to the background.

During my lifetime, one political example of that was Michael Harrington's *The Other America,* which was widely read in the 1960s. Harrington's thesis was that to middle- and upper-class Americans it was as though the poor did not exist because they had been allowed to recede so far into the background. Harrington pulled the background forward until poverty was right in front of people and therefore (for a time, at least) had to be faced. Today, we all intellectually know that poverty exists—globally, nationally, and within our own city— but a question we might ask ourselves is "Where does poverty exist for us? Does it exist in our foreground or in the background?" For most middle- and upper-class Americans, it requires intentionality—it requires the use of one's higher powers—to move other people's poverty from the background to our foreground. It is a human tendency to focus on whatever is immediate while overlooking that which is more distant for us.

III

I started thinking about backgrounds and foregrounds after walking around for a few days asking God what he was trying to teach me through the story of Jesus and Blind Bartimaeus. I was asking for a starting point, a toehold. Then an inner voice said to me, "Notice that Jesus is bringing Bartimaeus out of the background into the foreground. Notice, further, that Jesus often did that."

That is one way to look at this story. Jesus was on foot walking through Jericho, traveling from the villages of Galilee toward the resistance that awaited him in Jerusalem. The large crowd that followed Jesus through the town was enthusiastic and joyous, but I imagine Jesus being somewhat subdued inasmuch as he was already aware of the life-threatening dangers that awaited him. As Jesus and his disciples left Jericho, with the large crowd that was with him filling the road, a beggar named Bartimaeus who was hidden by the crowds began to call out to Jesus, saying, "Jesus, son of David, have mercy on me!" People in the crowd tried to shush Bartimaeus—they were doing their best to keep the blind beggar in the background— but he himself was determined to get into the foreground and shouted more loudly than before, "Jesus, son of David, have mercy on me!" Jesus, who might have paid attention only to those who were closest to him or who might have turned inward, preoccupied with worries about his own possible death, instead stopped, listened and said, "Call him here." Bartimaeus must have been some distance away. Otherwise, Jesus would have simply turned to Bartimaeus or would himself have called out to him. Instead, Jesus said to those who were closer to Bartimaeus, "Call him here." Jesus rescued Bartimaeus from the obscurity of the background and brought him front and center into the foreground where he healed him.

A similar incident occurs when Jesus is speaking to a smaller crowd somewhere in the Galilee. This time children who have been playing on the fringes of the crowd begin to move closer to Jesus. The disciples intercept them, hoping to keep them in the background, but Jesus doesn't want them in the background. Jesus wants the children in the foreground, so he invites them forward, where everyone can see them, and he says, "God's kingdom is only given to such as these."

Or again, Jesus was speaking to people who were caught up in the cares and anxieties of their own lives. As finite creatures they were concerned about their security—they were worried about having suitable clothes to wear and enough food to eat. Jesus addressed their worries by asking them to lift their eyes from the foreground to the background. He pointed beyond them and said, "Look at the lilies of the field; look at the birds of the air. How gloriously God provides for these." Jesus comforted them—he helped them to regain perspective—by drawing the natural background of their lives into the foreground.

IV

It occurs to me that we can learn a lot about people by noticing what they keep in the foreground and what they allow to recede into the background.

Recently I read *A Whole New Life* by Reynolds Price, who is a distinguished professor of English at Duke University and himself a prolific writer of novels, stories, essays and poems. In 1984 Price was walking across the Duke campus when he noticed that he could no longer lift his left foot the way he had always been able to. Soon he learned that a ten-inch long, pencil-thick cancer was wrapped around his spinal cord from his neck-hair downward. *A Whole New Life* tells the story of the painful, discouraging and paralyzing events that occurred afterwards. For four years the pain was excruciating and the limitations placed upon him were severe, as he fought to let go of his old life and create a new life as a pain-ridden paraplegic in a wheel chair. It is a book worth reading and you will marvel at Price's courage, strength of spirit and fortitude. If ever there was a formula for bitterness, this is one of them, but now, ten years later, Reynolds Price talks like this, even though his paralysis continues.

> A disaster? Yes, it was a disaster for me for a while—great chunks of four years. A catastrophe surely, a literally upended life with all parts strewn and some of the most urgent parts lost for good, within and without. But if I were called on to

value honestly my present life beside my past—I'd have to say that, despite an enjoyable fifty-year start, these recent years since full catastrophe have gone still better. They've brought more in and sent more out—more love and care, more knowledge and patience, more work in less time.

How did Price survive and now transcend this terrible period? First, by letting go of all he had lost and by allowing his pain and losses to recede into the background. Second, however altered or limited his possibilities were, he brought whatever possibilities still existed for him into the foreground of his daily life. He focused on who he was, rather than on who he had once been.

V

NOT ONLY CAN you tell a lot about a person by noticing what he puts in the foreground and what he allows to recede into the background, but we can also change the shape and quality of our own lives by exchanging background and foreground.

Last Tuesday evening, a mother and father and sixteen-year-old son were guests in the evening educational series in which we are trying to better understand issues surrounding homosexuality. I have been attending as a participant and it has been an important study for me, especially because we have been able to talk freely and honestly with people who have had to personally deal with homosexuality. The family that visited us last Tuesday was very open, very loving, and very Christian. The mother was especially well versed in the Scriptures. She told about the time two years ago when her then-fourteen-year-old son talked with her about knowing that he was homosexual. She had felt that that was a possibility for a long time. He had soft, sensitive qualities, and children in his school had chased him and called him "Faggot" as early as the third grade. She told us how, after her son had gone to school the next day, she cried and cried. "All I could think about were the many hateful stereotypes that I had been taught about homosexuals," she said. "It was so painful to me to have a son like that. But after several hours of crying and praying, God whispered to me. God said, 'You have always known that you have a wonderful son. You still have a wonderful son.'"

In my terms, then, she exchanged backgrounds and foregrounds. She herself put it this way.

> In a photograph I was looking at the face of my son whom I loved and I decided that rather than allow the hateful stereotypes I'd previously been taught about homosexuality to disfigure the face of my son, I would place the face of my son over the stereotypes I had been taught about homosexuality. I decided to let him give me new understandings of homosexuality, rather than allowing what I'd heard about homosexuality to change my love and respect for him.

I was very moved by this mother's decision, because I have known parents who have not chosen to do that, but have instead turned away from their children when their son or daughter allowed a similar truth about themselves to be known. Those parents focused so entirely on the hateful stereotypes, that they were no longer able to see the faces of their children and consequently pushed their children from the forefront into the background of their lives. Thus, my heart was warmed to see a mother who was able to keep, in the foreground of her life, the face of her own beloved son.

VI

ON THE ROAD from Jericho to Jerusalem, Jesus stopped and asked others to summon the blind beggar, Bartimaeus, so he could see him, and speak to him, and heal him. Jesus was able to do that because as a human being he had a great deal of flexibility and freedom with regard to who and what would be in the forefront and who and what would be in the background of his life. The Gospels relate many incidents in which Jesus stopped what he was doing to move someone who was in the background into the foreground—not only Bartimaeus and the children, but also a bent-over woman in the synagogue and a man with a withered hand—and a crooked tax collector up in a sycamore tree and ten lepers who were always supposed to stay in the background. We learn a lot about Jesus by noticing who he allowed to remain in the background and who he called into the foreground. We can also learn a lot about ourselves by noticing who or what we bring forward and who or what we allow to recede.

On what do you focus in life? What do you almost always notice? What do you rarely experience or see? Our lives, our characters, and our souls are shaped by whom or by what we place in our foreground. Right now, what in your life are you bringing forward? What are you pushing away or allowing to recede?

October 1994

Blind Spots

◆　◆　◆

> . . . have you not made distinctions among
> yourselves and become judges . . . ?
>
> — James 2:4

N THE BIBLE, faults and frailties of religious heroes and
ordinary Christians alike are frequently exposed and ad-
mitted. The Letter of James is striking in this regard. In the
letter's first chapter James reminds the church that in Jesus of
Nazareth and in the community that proclaimed him Lord,
God was intentionally working to create a new strain of human
beings—people who both internalized and lived their own
Christ-consciousness, thereby acting as a catalyst to raise human life to a new level of mercy, meaning, justice and love. But
here the second chapter has hardly begun when we see that in
one important respect the Christians to whom James is writing
don't look very new. When rich and prominent persons come
into their company, they fawn all over them, as if they had
never heard the story of Jesus Christ. They take them to the
best seat in the house and say, "Sit here, please." And when
poor people, dirty and shabbily dressed, enter their company—those poor to whom Jesus Christ himself was so frequently drawn—they say, "Ah, why don't you sit on the floor
here at my feet or outside under a tree—somewhere in the
back." What's more, they didn't even notice the contradic-
tion between their way and Jesus' way until James pointed it
out. It never occurred to them that they were expressing the
world's values rather than Christ's values. Where the rich and
poor in their midst were concerned, those early Christians had
a blind spot.

II

TWO BASIC IMAGES come to mind when I think of blind spots. I think first of the blind spots that sometimes appear in our rearview mirrors when we are trying to switch lanes on a freeway. On occasion, I have looked carefully in my rearview mirror and side mirrors and decided that the way was clear only to have someone lay on his horn when I turned on my blinker signal and began to move left. What a shock that is! Where did that car come from? I just looked back there! But the car was unseen by me—tucked inside my blind spot. That convinces me that blind spots exist and that they can be dangerous to ourselves and others.

A second image concerns the way our eyes are built. In the back of each of our eyes there is a spot where the optical nerve attaches to the retina. There is no room for any light receptors there and we are truly blind at that particular spot. Usually we don't notice, but under certain conditions we can see the effect of our blind spot. If I treat this as a parable and not merely as a biological fact, it occurs to me that you and I may develop blind spots at the very points that we are most attached or rooted. A strong opinion, a fervent hope, a personal bias, or a cherished belief may create blind spots. That happens in the Bible when King David becomes so attached to his fantasies about Bathsheba that he can no longer see that her husband, Uriah the Hittite, is his faithful soldier and friend. His attachment so blinds him that David cannot see that plotting to have Uriah killed in battle is a terrible sin.

Here are two contemporary examples of blind spots that are painful to me because I so admire both of these persons. The first concerns Wendell Berry whose writings and personal witness I appreciate very much. His concerns are many. He cares about the earth, the quality of human culture and human life, and about the economic decline in our small towns and rural areas. It bothers him that in so many communities young people have to move away in order to earn a living. But I was surprised to read an essay recently in which Wendell Berry was a strong advocate for the growing of tobacco as a regional industry. Knowing what we know now, tobacco seems a strange substance to be promoted by one who cares so much for the quality of human life, but Wendell Berry grew up in tobacco country. He does not see tobacco as I, an ex-smoker, do. And that is because the tobacco fields of Kentucky are one of the places in life to which he is strongly attached and is still rooted.

Mother Theresa of Calcutta is a Christian servant whose love for the poor, the dying and the outcast is legendary. She emanates compassion and love. I was surprised, therefore, to read in an interview with her that under no circumstances would she allow a starving child to be adopted by a woman who, at any time, had had an abortion. Since she epitomizes the mercy, love and forgiveness we have seen in Jesus Christ, that seemed to me a blind spot. I do not believe that Jesus Christ would forbid a woman who had had an abortion to mother a child. God certainly doesn't. But Mother Theresa would not even consider that. You may not agree, but I see that as a blind spot. It has to do with where she is rooted.

III

WE ALL HAVE blind spots. In human beings they are built in. I haven't talked about mine today, because I can't see them. Still, I know that they are there. They show up in dreams, sometimes. Or other people point them out to me. But what can we do about our blind spots, if we can't eliminate them? We can change our perspective. We can try to look at what we are doing from another point of view.

King David could not see how grievously he had wronged his friend and loyal officer, Uriah, when he stole his wife and had him killed. Then Nathan the prophet came and told King

David a story about a rich man with many flocks who stole the one lamb his neighbor owned and cherished. "What should happen to this greedy rich man?" the prophet Nathan asked. "He should be put to death," David said, indignant over the greedy rich man's cruelty. "You are that thief," said Nathan. "You are that man." Because Nathan tricked David into seeing his action from another point of view, David was exposed to his own blind spot.

Last spring I was driving to church one morning. Traffic was heavy and I was on the inside lane on Third Street half a mile east of here. Suddenly, the driver in the next lane swerved into my lane without warning. It was not a malicious, hostile act—the driver did not even see me. Apparently I was in a blind spot. But my own attempt to avoid the accident slammed me into the curb and ruined my wheel and wasted a couple hours of my time. Actually, I was fairly lucky. It could have been much worse. Now when I am thinking about switching lanes, I try to think about what it will do to any driver who may be hidden in my blind spot. I look much more carefully now. I signal longer before I move. I try to see my lane switching from the other driver's point of view.

When a lawyer asked Jesus, "Who is my neighbor?" Jesus told the story of a man who was robbed and beaten as he traveled the Jericho Road. Then Jesus described travelers who passed the injured man without helping him and, finally, a Samaritan traveler who did help him. Then Jesus changed the question. That is, he changed the point of view. He did not ask the lawyer, "Having heard that story, who do you think your neighbor is?" but "Who do you think looked like a neighbor to the man who had fallen among robbers?" When we are able to expand our vision so as to look at life, not only through our own eyes, but through the eyes of others—those who are at the side of the road having been robbed and beaten, those in the adjoining lane who have no idea what we are about to do, or the person whose spouse we are trying to steal—then we have a chance to compensate for our blind spots. By contrast, we may become a danger to ourselves and others if we look at life only through our own eyes—especially, if we are too attached, too dug in, too rooted.

September 1994

The All-You-Can-Eat Colander Diet

◆　◆　◆

They said to him. "Are we also blind?"

— John 9:40

SPENT MOST OF last week in Cambridge, Massachusetts, at a meeting of the World Future Society, which was considering the theme "Toward the New Millennium: Living, Learning and Working." It was one of those eight in the morning until ten o'clock at night conferences and I was exposed to far more information than I have yet been able to assimilate. So this is not a report—although I can say that many futurists are more humble than they used to be. They aren't as sure what's coming next. They are less confident about science and technology than they were in the past. Instead of making bold predictions about what will happen next week, they have shifted to talking about Chaos Theory and the Butterfly Effect and have developed increased interest in human values, spirituality, care of the human soul, and God. Many futurists are so beleaguered by reality's assault on their former predictions that I couldn't help but feel that their emerging interest in God smacked a bit of foxhole religion. Some futurists are already out in the galaxy somewhere announcing the next great leap in human evolution while others are more down to earth, truly alarmed by genocide in Rwanda, cholera in Zaire, the shortage of water worldwide, and violence in Bosnia and South Dallas.

What becomes clear when listening to the many voices at such a conference is that "The Future" doesn't exist as a single entity. Rather, we are headed toward a multiplicity of futures— yours, mine, Africa's—the future of those who have and those who have not—the future of those who will continue to expand their skills and capacities and the future of those who will not. One speaker warned that from now on those adults who stop learning will bring a quick end to their productive work life. However, I'm not wanting to report. Instead I'm wanting to share a few anecdotes from the World Future Conference until they lead us (as they eventually will) to today's reading of the ninth chapter of the Gospel of John. If, as we start out, you would be helped to know where we are going, I will remind you of Jesus' teaching that life is always more surprising than our model and that, therefore, it is spiritually important to be open to God's larger reality whenever it presents itself.

II

FIRST, AN IMAGE from The Far Side. In a workshop that was asking participants to look at life's issues and problems in new ways, the presenter projected a Gary Larsen cartoon onto a screen. For those who struggle with extra calories and their own lack of discipline, this looked like a binge-proof solution. It was called The All-You-Can-Eat Colander Diet and showed a man eating an ice cream cone through the metal colander that was strapped to his face. That's the solution! Eat as much as you want with the only stipulation being that you first shove whatever you are eating through the patterned holes in the colander that covers your face.

Immediately my thoughts jumped. I said, "This is not only the answer to overeating, but it is also an answer to the chaotic overload of information that is now overwhelming us. Today there is more life out there than we can comfortably take in. What we need is an All-You-Can-Eat-Colander Diet for our minds. We need a metal shield with itsy-bitsy patterned holes that we can strap over our minds!" Just then I heard the voice of Jesus speak. He said, "Nice idea, but you're too late. Most people already have a colander strapped over their minds."

III

ANOTHER WORKSHOP in Boston was led by a casual acquaintance whom I hadn't seen for thirty years. The last time I saw Bob Keck he was an urban minister in Des Moines, and I was an urban minister in Milwaukee, and we were having lunch in a Jewish Deli in New York during a meeting of the United Methodist Board of Global Ministries. I was struck by how healthy, vital and handsome Bob looked. He has aged more elegantly than I. When I reintroduced myself after his workshop he said, "I can tell that I haven't changed over the past thirty years, but what's happened to you?"

Actually a lot has happened to Bob as well as to me. In his mid-thirties he began to experience excruciating back pain and gradual crippling as the aftermath of polio and as a result of the metal screws used to straighten his spine when he was a child. Because his quality of life was rapidly deteriorating, Bob traveled to the Mayo Clinic in Rochester, Minnesota. There doctors told him that his pain was easily explained by his history and by his X-rays. Only two procedures offered the possibility of relief—either surgery, which in his case was not indicated, or powerful painkilling drugs. They told him that his crippling would increase, that he should plan to spend the rest of his life in a wheel chair, and sent him home with the powerful painkilling drugs. Those drugs never did control the pain completely, and over the next three years, the pain and crippling increased. Hoping that a breakthrough might have occurred over that three years, he went to the medical center at Southern Illinois University for another opinion. They repeated the prognosis. Surgery was contra-indicated. He would spend his life in a wheel chair, and they increased his daily dosage of the powerful painkilling drugs. Again, three more years later, when he could stand the pain no longer, Bob went to the medical center of Ohio State University, near where he was then living. There had been no breakthrough in medical science. The diagnosis and prognosis were the same. One doctor became angry with him. He said, "Bob, you have been to three of the best medical centers in the world. They all tell you the same thing and that isn't going to change. It's time you worked through your denial. You will always be in a wheelchair and you will always have severe pain. Here is the strongest pain medication we can give you." Bob felt that the gist of this third opinion was, "Please go home and don't bother us again."

Soon afterwards, a heretical thought arose in Bob's mind: "What if the experts didn't know everything?" Determined to try every available avenue, Bob began to explore as many alternative concepts of health and medicine as he could find. Slowly he designed his own healing regimen: stretching, exercise, a new diet, prayer, visualization, meditation, and chanting. He reexamined his personal goals and his attitudes toward life. He did whatever looked like it might somehow help him to walk again and little by little he healed.

Today Bob Keck is as healthy and mobile as you can be at 59 years of age. Part-time, he is a member of the faculty of the Ohio State Medical School, advising them about holistic approaches to medicine and mind-soul-body issues. In the group of men with whom he plays tennis are two of the physicians who told him he would never walk again. Bob says that he has a little extra adrenaline flowing on the days he plays them. The problem with experts, Bob concludes, is not that they don't know everything. We can't expect them to know everything. The problem with experts is that they don't know that they don't know everything. Instead of saying, "There is nothing in our discipline that can help you, but there is a Navajo medicine man whose chants are rumored to be effective," they say, "There is no hope for you." They think that their own little map of life is the territory.

IV

Now PERHAPS WE can turn to today's story from the Gospel of John. In Jerusalem on a Sabbath day, Jesus healed a man who had been born blind. Some of the onlookers who were experts about life didn't believe it. The fact that the man was born blind is significant. That makes it clear that the blindness was not emotionally caused—his was not an hysterical blindness. Presumably, to heal someone who had been born blind, something physical would have to be changed—dead optical nerves would have to be attached or activated—and all the experts knew that that couldn't possibly happen and had never happened in the history of the whole world—which simply means that it had never happened in their little cul-de-sac within the span of their own experience and memory—so they attacked the man who was now seeing for the first time and accused him of being a liar. "Why are you telling everyone you were born blind, when obviously you weren't?," they asked him. When his parents were found and testified that indeed their son had been born blind, the experts quickly dropped the subject and proceeded on the basis of what they also knew to be absolutely true—namely, that God did no work (even healing work) on the Sabbath. Therefore, because he had healed on the Sabbath, Jesus was undoubtedly a sinner. The experts were so locked into their model of the way life ought to be, that they couldn't believe their own ears and eyes, which made them the ones who were deaf and blind. In my imagery, they had a colander with itsy-bitsy holes strapped over their minds and if reality didn't fit the pattern they had spent their lives creating, they couldn't take in the new information. The colander over their minds prevented them from receiving God's larger reality.

V

ONE OF THE MOST encouraging of the presentations that I attended at the World Future Conference was entitled "Creating Organizations that Learn." It was presented by two bright, enthusiastic, and courteous young executives from Electronic Data Systems (EDS) which is now a subsidiary of General Motors. EDS has 75,000 employees worldwide and is working with the Organizational Learning Center at MIT in an effort to create a corporation that is able to learn and change faster than today's external environment.

Given my thoughts about All-You-Can-Eat Colander Diets for the mind, I was very interested when Renee Moorefield, the young woman who coordinates the Learning Project at EDS, described how they began the process. They began, she said, by assuming that each of the individuals taking part was inevitably viewing the world through a grid, pattern, or map, model, or (as futurists like to say) paradigm that they had previously strapped over their minds. We all have assumptions about life, she said. Some are helpful and some are not so helpful, but the first step in learning and growing is to tear those assumptions away from our eyes, so that we can look at them, and examine them, and ask how they are or are not working for us and how we might benefit from changing them. This is hard work, requiring patience and courage, she said. The assumptions through which we view life have their maximum power to limit or deceive us when we don't even know that they are there.

VI

AT THE CLOSE of today's Gospel lesson a strange exchange takes place between Jesus and the no-longer-blind man. Jesus said: "I came into the world . . . so that those who do not see may see." The expert onlookers who overheard him asked: "Are you saying that WE are blind?"

Jesus answered, "If you knew you were blind, I could help you; but I can't do a thing for you as long as you are certain that you see."

Last week in Boston a friend and I were browsing in Quincy Market and decided to walk up to the North End to see Old North Church where Paul Revere once waited for the signal "One if by land; two if by sea." My friend wanted to ask directions, but I said, "I was there twenty years ago. We don't need directions. It's this way." A woman who had overheard our conversation asked, "Where are you going?" "To Old North Church," I answered. "Then you'd better turn around," she said, "because you are walking in the opposite direction."

Jesus understood that life is always more complex and surprising than our map or model. We all view life through a grid or a filter. We are in the greatest danger of getting lost in those very hours when we are most certain that we can see. Being open to the possibility that we do not now know every-thing—even (or especially) in the areas in which we believe ourselves to be expert—is the first step in redemption. Blessed are those who understand that they do not fully see. God can work with them.

July 1994

The High Cost of Knuckling Under

◆　◆　◆

Do not be conformed to this world.

—Romans 12:2

THE MOST PERSONALLY helpful book that I read during the past year was *Cancer as a Turning Point* by Lawrence LeShan. The book was written for cancer patients and their families, but I found it stimulating although I am not aware of any malignancy within my own body. I read the book as preventive medicine.

Early in *Cancer as a Turning Point,* LeShan tells the story of a Brazilian physician whom he identifies simply as Maria. Maria, married and the mother of twin girls, loved her work as a pediatrician in Rio de Janeiro. But her husband, who was trained and employed as an engineer, hated his work. He wanted to be a poet. Her daughters, both showing talent for the theater, wanted to leave Brazil and move to London. Maria acquiesced. First she agreed to support the family financially so that her husband could write poetry. Then she agreed to move to London for her daughters' sake. The job she had been promised in pediatrics fell through. To keep everyone supported in the manner to which they had become accustomed, she entered an oncology partnership, which she very much disliked. She also missed the beaches, the climate, the people and the customs of Rio de Janeiro. She never felt at home in London and missed speaking Portuguese. After a few years in London she noticed a lump in her breast. An examination showed that cancer had spread widely. Her prognosis was poor and surgery was not an option.

Maria's story caused me to recall these words of the Apostle Paul from his Letter to the Romans:

> Do not be conformed to this world,
> but be transformed by the renewal of your mind,
> that you may prove what is the will of God,
> what is good, acceptable, and perfect.

II

THIS INSTRUCTION FROM the Apostle Paul has a way of bringing out whatever is left of the rebellious adolescent in me. Perhaps because Paul's message is cast in the form of a "Thou shalt not," something within me wants to resist it. Because of my rebellion, I mistakenly think that Paul is trying to deprive me of something by urging me not to be conformed to this world.

My resistance would surprise Paul. He did not think that he was sharing bad news, but good news. He wasn't trying to deprive us of something, but to give us something. Paul was offering the followers of Christ a liberating possibility—namely, the opportunity of not being conformed to this present world.

Jesus has always been a model for me in this regard. Clearly, he did not submit to his world's dominant value system. Jesus lived at a time when the upper or ruling classes were enormously wealthy and enjoyed great luxury and splendor. He himself was born into a small middle class with no special disadvantages. Nevertheless, rather than aspiring to the riches of those who were above him, he chose to identify with and care for the masses of poor, outcast, and oppressed whom society ranked below him. He turned his back on the comfort that the world thought important in order to pursue what he thought was important.

Since boyhood, I have dwelled on the fact that Jesus chose to give himself to the outcast and the poor. What I am viewing as important now is not only the particular path that Jesus chose for himself, but the underlying fact that Jesus did choose a path for himself. Instead of knuckling under to the values, standards and idols of others—even the religious values that surrounded him—he lived the way he believed God was calling him.

More and more I believe that what was true of Jesus of Nazareth can also be true of us. I believe that God is also calling us to live a life that is in harmony with the gifts, capacities, interests and passions that God has placed within us. When Paul says, "Do not be conformed to this world," he is also saying "Don't spend all your time, energy, and money living somebody else's agenda for your life, but break free from that as Jesus did." I don't take that to mean "Do your own thing!" or "Honor every whim!" or "Pursue every desire!" Instead, I hear Paul warning us against allowing ourselves to be defined by other people, or by circumstances or by our surrounding culture. I hear Paul calling us to be our own most true, most authentic, most God-given selves.

III

BUT HOW DO we keep from being conformed? How do we keep from being captured by the whims of our surrounding culture, from being a slave to someone else's value system, or from knuckling under? There is a clue in the second clause of Paul's message: "Do not be conformed to this world, but be transformed by the renewal of your mind . . . "

To "renew our mind" is to regain our right senses. It is to wake up and become conscious. It means coming out of our confusion. It means honestly looking at our life, asking ourselves where we're headed and deciding whether we really want to continue in the direction we are going. It also means getting in touch with any renewing energies that may still exist within us. Unfortunately, often we do not pause for such an honest assessment until there is a collapse in our life—either in our external circumstances or within our minds or bodies.

When Lawrence LeShan met Maria she was in deep despair—about her job, about her cancer which was rampant and
considered terminal, and about the fact that she would not
long be able to provide financially for her daughters and
husband as they had all become accustomed. For a long time
LeShan just listened to Maria. Then he sat with her in silence
and shared her sorrow. Finally, because he was soon to leave
London, he hurried his treatment by telling her this story.
These are his words:

> I told Maria the story of the woman who was sunbathing
> nude. A lovely chickadee flew down and perched on her
> ankle. She smiled lovingly at it. Then a great orange-and-
> black butterfly alighted on her knee. Again she smiled warmly.
> A magnificent dragonfly with its iridescent wings settled on
> her shoulder. It also received a welcoming smile, as did a
> beautiful goldfinch that came down and perched on her toes.
> Then a mosquito came down, settled on her breast, and bit
> her. She looked at it and said, "All right. Everybody off!"

At the punchline, Maria laughed loudly. Then she sat quietly,
apparently thinking. Finally, a grin crossed her face and she
asked, "Do you think I really could?"

The change was not easy, but neither was it impossible. In
fact, others helped her more than she thought they would.
That very night she called a family meeting. She told her
husband and daughters that while her prognosis was poor she
wanted to live. She said that her chances of living would
improve if she could design a life she really felt was worth
living. She asked her husband to return to work. Many poets
had written their poems after eight hours of other work, she
said. She told her children that they would be returning to the
public school. Acting lessons were still possible, if they found
part-time jobs to pay for them. The maid would have to go, so
there was need for all to pitch in. Maria herself would be
resigning her oncology position in order to update her pediat-

rics skills through a yearlong residency. They would stay in London for now, but returning to Brazil was still a future possibility.

Four years had passed at the time of writing. Maria had been a pediatrician for three years, earning far less than she had as an oncologist but enjoying her work much more. Her husband had found a low-level engineering job that was relatively undemanding. He wrote at night and had published two volumes of poems. The twins had worked part-time to continue acting classes, had done a few commercials, and had acted in small avant-garde theaters in London. Each summer Maria vacationed in Rio de Janeiro. Because money was short, she traveled alone. Maria's chemotherapy had gone better than expected. Her tumors had shrunk, but not disappeared. When the book was published, her condition was stable but guarded. Maria had already outlived her prognosis by several years.

For twenty-five years, Lawrence LeShan has worked with terminally ill cancer patients. His key insight has been this:

> In a large majority of the people I saw (certainly not all), there had been previous to the first noted signs of cancer, a loss of hope in ever achieving a way of life that would give real and deep satisfaction, that would provide a reason for living, the kind of meaning that makes us glad to get out of bed in the morning and glad to go to bed at night—the kind of life that makes us look forward zestfully to each day and to the future.

Knuckling under to a life others have designed for us; staying trapped in situations that diminish us; living without hope or satisfaction can literally take the life right out of us.

Paul's additional insight is that such a life—conforming to the world—being driven this way and that by the values and standards of others—is what happens when our mind is not renewed—that is, when we're not thinking. Our lives begin to be transformed—our lives begin to be our lives—when we start thinking. We don't have to choose to be conformed to this world. That just happens to us when we're not thinking—when we're not asking questions like "What do I really want from my life?" "Is the way I am now living worth the price I'm having to pay?" "What way of living would be most satisfying and most authentic for me?" and "Is this the life to which God is calling me?"

IV

THERE'S MORE: "Do not be conformed to this world, but be transformed by the renewal of your minds, that you may prove what is the will of God, what is good, acceptable and perfect."

Paul asks us to "prove" the will of God. "Proving" here means "checking it out" or "demonstrating"—not by thinking about it, nor arguing about it, but by living it. We prove that God's intention for our life is acceptable and good by living it. Here are two suggestions that I believe will help us to discover for ourselves the goodness of God's will in our own life.

My first suggestion is this: Believe that a life which is in harmony with who you actually are is available to you.

Among terminal cancer patients LeShan has found many who did not believe that they had "their own song to sing." Even if they did, such patients often feared that no one else would want to hear their song, or that they couldn't make a living singing it, or that so singing would somehow drive people off and erode their human relationships. This, in part, was why they lost hope of ever living a life that was wonderfully satisfying to them. They feared that the only way to survive was to be who they weren't. They mistakenly believed that the safest thing to do was to knuckle under. In response to that fear, LeShan says:

> In more than twenty-five years . . . I have seen these reactions
> many times. Yet I have never seen a single person who, upon
> finding his or her own song or style, still felt the same. With
> all the people with whom I have worked, their own song was

one that was acceptable to themselves and others, was possible to play fully in this culture (and to make a living at when this was necessary), and increased their human relationships and made them more fulfilling. I have never seen an exception to this.

My second suggestions is this: Begin immediately searching for that life. Right now. Start intentionally building that life.

The key question LeShan urges terminally ill cancer patients to ask is, "What style of being or living or creating would bring me to a life of zest, enthusiasm and involvement? What kind of life would energize me and make me want to get up in the morning? What do I personally want?" He also asks patients to focus not on what is wrong in their life but on what is right—for instance, "What are the special and unique God-given qualities that are within me to which I might give more expression?"

"Searching for this kind of life," says LeShan, "mobilizes the immune system against cancer more than anything else we know today." Some of us have strayed so far from our path that if someone asked us, "What kind of life would bring you enthusiasm and zest?," our honest answer would be, "I don't know." Incredibly, we don't need to know in order to improve our life. All we need is the desire and the determination to know. Speaking of cancer patients again, LeShan says: "Remarkably, simply committing oneself to this search can have a positive effect on one's immune system—even before the answer is found." The important thing is committing ourselves to finding and building that kind of life.

V

"DO NOT BE conformed to this world," says Paul, "but be transformed by the renewal of your minds"—that is, by thinking about your life and re-committing yourself to find and build your own most appropriate life. Here's what a famous

Christian from a former time—the Seer of Lublin—had to say. For me it also points the way to increasing the rewards of our life while reducing the high costs of knuckling under:

> It is impossible to tell other individuals the way they should take. For one way to serve God is through learning, another through prayer, another through fasting, and still another through eating. Everyone should carefully observe what way his heart draws him to, and then with all his strength choose this way.

I personally believe that God has given each of us a song to sing and that we are most faithful and most alive when, in the midst of our circumstances, we discover and sing it. The first step toward health of any kind is deciding that we will do our best to discover and sing our own most personal song, rather than knuckling under.

November 1990

Roots, Vines, and Branches

◆　◆　◆

I am the real vine, and my Father is the gardener.

—John 15:1

W HEN JESUS SAID, "I am the vine, you are the branches,"
he was speaking to people sufficiently familiar with
vines and branches to extract lots of their own
meaning from that metaphor. My own knowledge of the plant
world is slight, so my understanding of this passage was given
a boost when a horticulturist stepped into my office one
morning last week while I was pondering this text.

This particular horticulturist steps into my office every
Thursday morning. I am referring to Al Morrison, a longtime
member of St. Mark's, who shares his time, concern, and
knowledge in caring for all the plants here at the church. Most
of the indoor plants here are Al's. He has grown them and cared
for them for many years. I'm not sure that I have ever kept a
houseplant alive longer than six months. By contrast, one of
the plants in my office is over thirty years old. That's because Al
is taking care of it. Each Thursday morning Al goes from room
to room watering the plants with rainwater he has collected
from his roof and taking any other measures he deems necessary. This week he also worked outside trimming the forsythia
bushes. Anyway, I was puzzling over this passage when Al
walked in and I had sense enough to know that God had sent
me a consultant, so I said "Al, I need some ideas. Talk to me
about pruning vines and branches." Al obliged, but before I tell
you what he said, let me share what I had been thinking about
before Al stepped into my office.

II

"I AM THE VINE, you are the branches," said Jesus. When I read those words, they triggered a memory. I left the present and was transported back in time to 1977. I was living then in Irvington, on the east side of Indianapolis, with my son, Matt. Matt was seven at the time. That was a difficult period—both for me and for Matt. Because of a divorce we had both been uprooted—Matt from his home, his church, his neighborhood, his friends, his baseball team, his school and his mother. We were trying to settle into a new life about ten miles across town from where we had lived before. That's not so far in miles, but when United Methodist ministers leave a place, they are expected to cut ties. Most of our support system was gone. So both for Matt and for me it was a difficult time. One night after I thought Matt was asleep I heard him crying in his room. I went in, sat on his bed and asked what was wrong. "I feel like a plant," Matt said, "whose root is still all the way back on New Jersey Street." I swallowed to push back my own tears and said, "So do I, Matt. So do I."

What Matt was saying was not simply that he felt a long way from home, but that he was so far from his root—so far from where he had once been planted—that he wasn't able to draw water and nutrients from that root all the way across town. At that distance he was not being nourished by the root, but was, as we say, dying on the vine. That's when I decided to break a rule and enrolled him on his old baseball team at the church we were supposed to leave behind. That wasn't the whole answer, of course. We needed to get replanted, but that helped in the transition. At the very least my son learned that I cared more about him than about some rule.

Here's another example that came to mind as I pondered this text. It's not about plants, but for me is a related metaphor. In the introduction to his book, *The Kingdom Within*, John Sanford describes the old well that served the needs of his family when he spent his childhood summers in an old farm-house in New Hampshire. Because of its depth the well was unusually reliable. Even during times of drought—even when neighbors' wells ran dry—this well faithfully yielded clear, cold water. Eventually, when the family fortunes improved, modern plumbing and running water were installed. At that time the old well was sealed. Several years later, moved by curiosity, John Sanford reopened the old well. As he removed the cover, he expected to see the same dark, cool, moist depths he had known as a boy. He was shocked to find the well bone dry. He tells the rest of the story like this:

> It took many inquiries on our part to understand what had happened. A well of this kind is fed by hundreds of tiny underground rivulets along which seeps a constant supply of water. As water is drawn from the well, more water moves into it along the rivulets, keeping those tiny apertures clear and open. But when such a well is not used and the water is not regularly drawn, the tiny rivulets close up. Our well, which had run without failing for so many years, was dry not because there was no water but because it had not been used.

Our souls are like that, Sanford went on to say. The fact that we are dry and depleted does not mean that there is no source of Living Water. It may be that we have been cut off from the source by our failure to keep drawing from the well.

So that's what I was thinking about before Al came in. The problem isn't that there are no spiritual refreshments and nutrients available in life. If we are depleted, that may be because we ourselves have neglected to lower our bucket. If we are withering on the vine, that may be because we have put too much distance between ourselves and our roots. What might we do, I was beginning to ask, to reconnect with our depths? What might we do to get closer to our roots? How might we reopen ourselves to the spiritual resources God gives? Those were the questions I was asking before Al stepped in. "Al, I need some ideas; talk to me about pruning vines and branches," I said.

III

I ASKED ABOUT pruning because of these words of Jesus Christ:

> I am the real vine, and my Father is the gardener. He breaks
> off every branch in me that does not bear fruit, and he prunes
> every branch that does bear fruit, so that it will be clean and
> bear more fruit.

Pruning, Al said, is cutting off or cutting back branches—either
a little or a lot. There are several reasons for pruning.

One big reason is the one mentioned in the Bible—produc-
tivity. If a particular branch isn't bearing any fruit—even after
it has been encouraged to do so—it makes sense to cut that
branch off. It is not only using water and nutrients but it is
using sunshine and taking up space. You can get lots more
production by cutting off the fruitless branch and encouraging
a more fruitful one to grow into that sunlight and space.

Even a fruitful branch will benefit from being cut back.
Pruning accelerates growth and fruitfulness because the end of
the branch where growth occurs will be closer to the nutrients
and water that are supplied by the vine and the root. Jesus says
that God prunes every branch that does bear fruit so that it will
bear even more fruit.

According to Al, gardeners also prune branches when they
are growing in the wrong direction. They cut the branch back
and thereby give it another chance to grow in the right direction. In this spirit, gardeners also prune in order to shape a
plant. It is by pruning that a gardener can help a plant to
achieve its desired potential.

Then Al summarized by saying that the gardener prunes a
plant to encourage the plant to do something that it isn't
doing. If it's a shade tree, the gardener prunes in order to get
more shade. If it's a flowering plant, the gardener prunes to get
more flowers. If it's a vine or a fruit tree, the gardener prunes to
increase the harvest. In short, the gardener prunes to bring the
plant into fuller harmony with the plant's intended purpose.

Pruning is not something that the plant does to itself, I noted. Pruning is what a plant that is cared for experiences at the hands of the gardener.

IV

AFTER AL LEFT my office I saw that this passage can be interpreted at two separate levels. The first level has to do with staying connected to the vine and close to the root. In our spiritual life, for example, we may neglect prayer or worship or meditation or service or study until one day we find that we no longer have spiritual interest, zeal or energy. In our daily work, we may, over a number of years, perform our tasks in a routine, halfhearted way, losing track of what creates excitement in us, until one day we find that our workplace is not a garden but a desert and that we are pumping from a painfully dry well. In a love relationship we may gradually allow ourselves to drift farther and farther away from our partner until one day we discover that we have completely lost touch with the joyous spontaneity that we formerly knew. "I am the real vine—you are the branches—without me you can do nothing," Jesus said to his disciples. Thus would I urge you to keep track of the sources of your energy. What gives you life? What equips you to persevere? What makes every effort worth it? What nourishes and refreshes your soul? What must you do to stay close to the sources of your life? This is the first level of meaning.

There is a second level here. That's the one to which Al was so sensitive. "I am the real vine," said Jesus, "and my Father is the gardener." That's the deeper level—"my Father is the gardener."

To be frank, I'm not sure that I want a gardener. I want to be in charge. I want to decide whether I will grow, and when I will grow and the direction in which I will grow. I want to be my own gardener! I don't even like haircuts and delay getting them as long as I can. I certainly don't want to be pruned by the Eternal on any regular basis. I don't want to be a project in God's garden. I want to grow in my own peculiar way.

But that's the rub. I may not, in fact, be growing in my own peculiar way. I may, as the Bible says, be "missing the mark." I may not be becoming the person I most truly could be and am. I may not be fulfilling the unique life forces that are within me. And it may be—notice that I'm being tentative here—that in order to come to fruition I do need the gardener's seemingly harsh interventions from time to time.

Still, it is always painful to have one of my dreams trimmed or one of my dead branches broken off. I suffer when a life direction to which I have been attached is turned aside or cut back. I don't like it when life says to me, "This is not the way!" or "You cannot continue as you are!" or "You must accept the unwanted!" or "Push has come to shove and you must now change your life!" I hate it when that happens. And yet it happens in my life, as it does in yours, time after time.

There is, I believe, a very important sense in which we are meant to be our own gardener. We have responsibility to manage our lives and tend our own souls. It is our job to stay close and connected to whatever are the sources of our life.

Yet there is another sense in which we are not the gardener. Day by day our lives are influenced and shaped by forces of which we are not conscious and which we do not control. Sometimes those forces bring pain, hardship and suffering—frustrating our plans and redirecting our life.

Jesus dared to attribute some of those intervening forces to God. Jesus said: My Father is the gardener. He breaks off every branch in me that does not bear fruit, and he prunes every branch that does bear fruit, so that it will be clean and bear more fruit. This is an aspect of God which we moderns have neglected and may resist, but it is a truth which the ancients knew. Five hundred years before Christ, the Greek poet Aeschylus saw that it is often through the painful, unwanted experiences in life that we grow. For example, he saw and said this:

> He who learns must suffer
> and even in his sleep
> pain that will not forget
> falls drop by drop upon the heart
> and in our despair
> and against our will
> comes wisdom
> by the awful grace of God.

Having also heard from Jesus Christ, we might paraphrase Aeschylus a bit:

> He who would grow must suffer
> and even in his sleep
> pain that will not forget
> falls drop by drop upon the heart
> and in our despair
> and against our will
> comes new more abundant life
> by the awful grace of God.

That is the deeper level—the more mysterious level—of this passage. In life there is a gardener. Because the gardener cares—because the gardener wants each plant to achieve its full potential—the gardener moves against the plant from time to time. For the sake of final fruitfulness, the gardener limits and intervenes.

April 1991

Laying Hold of God

◆　◆　◆

Jacob said, "I will not let you go unless
you bless me."
　　　　　　　　　　　— Genesis 32:26

HERE ARE TWO things I have learned—one from preaching and the other from living. I have learned from preaching that it is impossible to speak the whole truth all at once. No matter what you say, it will be incomplete and, therefore, a distortion. From living, I have learned that it is possible to err in every direction. Regardless of the direction in which we are moving, it is possible to go too far in that direction. Therefore, I find it helpful to know my biases—to be aware of the directions in which I habitually travel and lean, so I am not enticed into further excesses, but have a fighting chance to counterbalance them. What I find challenging about speaking to a group of people is that they aren't all leaning in the same direction. What frees one may further entrap another. These words are intended for those who don't normally approach God the way Jacob did. I don't normally approach God the way Jacob did.

II

I WAS TAUGHT to approach God the way Peter approached Jesus when he said, "Lord, depart from me for I am a sinful man." Peter was kneeling in the dirt in that moment with his arms tightly wrapped around the legs of Jesus. That is what is known as a double message. My mental picture of that story of Peter huddled at Jesus' feet somehow reminds me of the comedian

Steve Martin, whom I saw in concert some years ago during the period in which Steve Martin enjoyed encouraging people to "get small." I don't remember why he said that, but every now and then he would interrupt his routine and say, "Let's get small," and the audience would laugh hilariously and people would scrunch down in their sets, trying to get very small. In that same spirit, when I was young I somehow embraced the notion that the best way to get God's attention was to get small, helpless, needy, guilty, or exceedingly pathetic. Just yesterday a woman who must have been reared in a similar decade and environment said to me, "I know that we must get very low before God will listen to us and help us."

Within the Church there are voices that encourage this impression. Is it not written, "A broken and contrite heart, O God, thou wilt not despise"? One of the places I learned to get small was in the traditional prayers that we repeated during the Sacrament of Holy Communion. Prayers like this:

> Almighty God, Father of our Lord Jesus Christ, maker of all things, judge of all men: we acknowledge and bewail our manifold sins and wickedness which we from time to time most grievously have committed, by thought, word, and deed, against thy divine majesty. We do earnestly repent and are heartily sorry for these our misdoings: the remembrance of them is grievous unto us . . .

Or in this "Prayer of Humble Access" which as a youth and young adult I dearly loved:

> We do not presume to come to this thy table, O merciful Lord, trusting in our own righteousness, but in thy manifold and great mercies. We are not worthy so much as to gather up the crumbs under thy table, but thou art the same Lord whose property is always to have mercy . . .

"Before God," said Soren Kierkegaard, "we are always in the wrong" and that kind of thinking has helped to shape Christian rituals, suggesting that unworthiness is the gateway to

God—that unworthiness is the posture which gains God's instant approval—and, finally, that unworthiness is the manipulative tool with which we best extract God's mercy and gifts. The story of Jacob's wrestling match with an angel reveals that unworthiness is not the only posture with which we may approach God.

III

JACOB WAS A twin—Rebekah and Isaac's second born—who exited the womb a moment after his brother, Esau. Tradition tells us that Jacob was clinging to Esau's heel as he entered the world, even then using Esau to gain momentum. While Esau was physically stronger, Jacob was the brains of the outfit. He gained by cleverness—some would say by trickery and deceit—what he could not have obtained straightforwardly. He schemed circles around his brother and likewise fooled his blind and dying father so as to receive the family's birthright for himself. Later, Jacob was cheated and deceived by Laban, his future father-in-law, allowing himself to be taken advantage of for the love of a woman. Before that part of the story ended, Jacob invented a clever way to trick Laban out of his strongest flocks, so that when the son-in-law and father-in-law finally parted, Jacob was prosperous and Laban was less so. All this happened before Jacob met God in the night. I'm not implying that Jacob was all bad, but want to make it clear that he was not all good. Jacob was crafty and ambitious—a survivor, a wheeler-dealer, a player. Not my kind of guy. Nevertheless, God loved him.

IV

ON THE NIGHT in question Jacob was alone in the countryside beside a river. He had sent his family and servants and flocks on ahead. Jacob was apprehensive. On the following day he was to meet Esau for the first time since he had defrauded him years before. Esau was still physically strong. He was also militarily strong and had four hundred men with him. Awaiting the confrontation, Jacob was thinking about his past—about things he might have done differently—just as you and I sometimes reflect on our past when we awake in the night. And in the darkness of that night, a man came to Jacob's campsite and began wrestling with him.

By "man" the writer of Genesis meant "angel" and by angel the writer was saying "God." That's how Jacob himself understood what was happening. Later he would say, "I was face to face with God!" Here is a less than perfect man—a sometimes deceitful and crafty man—who is recalling the major lie on which his life is built when God comes to him at night. However, Jacob doesn't play dead. Jacob doesn't curl up in a ball and whimper. Rather than beg for mercy, Jacob lays hold of God and wrestles with him. Jacob says, "I've got you now," and fights back. Jacob fights so fiercely that at daybreak the angel (that is, God) wants to escape. He says, "Let me go." And Jacob says, "No, I won't let you go until you bless me." The angel threw Jacob's hip out of joint so that each time he limped he would remember who was Jacob and who was God, but the angel did bless him. Get it? Crafty, tricky Jacob grabbed hold of God and hung on until God blessed him. God blessed him not because Jacob was perfect, but because he was gutsy and persistent. A precise translation is useful. The angel said:

> You shall no longer be called Jacob, but Israel, for you have striven with God and with humans, and have prevailed. (Genesis 32:28)

You know what it means to prevail, don't you? It means to be still standing when the dust has settled and many others have fallen. It means to be bloody but unbowed, even if you have a few scars, your hip is out of joint, and you noticeably limp. One can't prevail without a degree of inner toughness. People who prevail are spiritual equivalents of junk yard dogs.

V

THERE ARE MANY ways to approach God. Peter's way—"Depart from me, Lord, for I am a sinful man"—is one way and I am sure that there are occasions in life when that way is the most appropriate. However, Jacob's way has merit, too, even though we have not had much schooling in it. Jacob's way is this: "I'm not perfect, God, but here I am. Yes, I have slipped and faltered and cut more corners than I might. Nevertheless, I am a reasonably worthwhile human being. What's more, I've paid my dues. I need you and I want your blessing. Therefore, I'm going to hang on to you and not let you go."

God responded to that. God did bless Jacob. Indeed, God made Jacob the father of the twelve tribes of Israel, not because he was perfect but because he had proven himself to be persistent and tough. Furthermore, that may be an appropriate way for us to pray, if we have a habit of getting small or weak whenever we draw near to God. "I've got you now," Jacob said to God in the night. And God blessed Jacob, because he stood up for himself, fought back, and was tenacious.

August 1993

Elephants in Our Living Room

◆　◆　◆

Do not let the sun go down on your anger.

— Ephesians 4:31

M Y MOST POPULAR sermon this summer—in terms of the number of comments it received—was the one that I didn't preach. More than a month ago I was walking through the church office when our secretary asked me for a sermon title two weeks ahead of time. That was asking quite a lot since as far as sermons are concerned I tend to live from week to week. But a title popped into my mind and I gave it to her so that it could be published in the newspaper. That title was "Elephants in Our Living Room." When it was actually time to write a sermon on that theme, I found that I was speechless and changed my topic to "The Hole in Life's Bucket," assuming that no one would notice such a minor switch. But lots of folks did. At the door that Sunday and in individual encounters over the next few weeks, people kept asking me, with a bit of an edge in their voice, "What happened to those elephants in our living room?" I explained that "elephants in the living room" is a metaphor for large issues that sometimes enter peoples lives—issues that everyone is aware of but no one talks about—and that I had been faithful to those elephants by not talking about them. This answer didn't seem to satisfy, so I'm back for another try.

Here's an extreme example of what I am talking about. If I showed up for worship some Sunday morning obviously drunk—if I stumbled around, slurred my speech and illustrated my sermon with crude humor, looking like Tom Hanks in the first reel of *A League of Their Own* and everybody noticed but nobody said anything, that would be what I mean by an elephant in the living room. If no one mentioned the inappropriateness of my behavior, if you did not call me to account and demand an apology and a penance of some important kind, our relationship would never be restored. Even though my behavior was never mentioned, it would have tremendous impact on any future interactions between us. We would soon find that an elephant that size refuses to be swept under a rug. I don't mean to say that if we just talked about what happened, we could automatically get that incident behind us—rapport would be very difficult to reestablish—but I am saying that our relationship could only get worse if we didn't talk about something that big which was bothering both of us. We would have a hard time shaking hands, looking each other in the eye or praying together with an elephant that size squatting on the floor between us.

II

SUCH ELEPHANTS TEND to congregate in those living rooms where people dread confronting one another or are afraid not to be nice. Sometimes such people forge a nonverbal contract that goes like this: I agree not to mention the elephant you dragged into the living room, if you agree not to mention mine. I'm sure you can see how, over time, such an agreement can lead to a very crowded, substandard living space. Unfortunately, the more elephants there are in a living room, the harder it is to mention them. Life would unfold more easily, if people dared to mention aloud the first elephant they saw—as in, "Honey, is that your elephant in the living room?" The saddest aspect of this is that some people who try to be nice, keep their lips zipped until the very last minute. So as not to stir up trouble or hurt anybody's feelings, they keep quiet as long as they can, until one day they say, "Sorry, Sweetheart, but I'm out of here—I can't stand the squeeze and the stench!" We're asking for future trouble if we don't mention the first elephant in the living room. (Here I am suddenly recalling a cartoon in which a bride and groom were driving off from the church a few minutes after their wedding. People were still waving, smiling and throwing rice; on the side of the car a "Just Married" sign was flapping; and inside the groom was reaching for the radio to tune in a Saturday afternoon baseball game. Rather than pretending not to notice, the bride looked at the groom and said, "That's one!") Many people would be happier today, if they had mentioned the first elephant in their living room.

Before continuing, I want to defend myself a bit and say that if Jesus could talk about lost coins under a couch, weeds in a wheat field, ten foolish virgins waiting for a man at midnight, new wine in an old skin, salt in the soup, leaven in the lump, a cow in a ditch and a blind man fallen into a pit—then I think it's OK for me to talk about elephants in a living room. Further, Jesus sought to bring things that were hidden out into the light. He asked people questions like "What do you want me to do for you?" and "Why are you so angry with me?" and "Do you really want to get well?" In today's scripture lesson, wanting to discover what people were saying about him behind his back, he asked, "Who do people say that I am?" He also asked Peter, "Who do you say that I am?" While there were times when Jesus favored secrecy, more generally he favored an open approach to life.

I recall once speaking at length with a college student who was grieving the end of a long-term love relationship. His pain was increased because he had thought things were going OK, and he hadn't seen the end coming. His partner had a list of unexpressed disappointments and grievances—changes that she was convinced he wouldn't have been able to make. Rather than talking with him about the ways in which she was disappointed, she left the relationship. "There were changes I could have made and would have been willing to make," he said. "Because she didn't talk to me, she didn't really know what was or wasn't negotiable. I would have appreciated a chance to make adjustments."

Likewise, I remember a divorced middle-aged man attempting to build a new life with a woman who also had been divorced. They had a lot in common, and he cared for her as much as she cared for him, but their relationship wasn't perfect. One of her habits drove him up a wall, but so as not to offend her, he never mentioned it. When he told me what was bothering him, the behavior he disliked seemed a minor matter—something that might have been easily modified—but he chose to view it as the tip of an iceberg, a foreshadowing of irreconcilable differences. Rather than expressing his discomfort and giving the woman a chance to respond, so as not to hurt her feelings he said that he hadn't yet healed from his divorce and left the relationship.

In both these instances the attempt to spare another person's feelings caused more injury than mentioning the disappointments would have done.

III

CONSIDER THIS COUNTER example. On the last night of Jesus' life, as Jesus was being accused by authorities inside Ciaphas' house, the disciple Peter was outside around the fire. He was recognized by a servant woman as having been with Jesus. Because of fear, Peter three times denied that he knew Jesus, as Jesus had predicted he would. Moreover, on the third occasion Jesus was being brought out onto the porch; he heard Peter's denial and their eyes met; but there was no way to talk about what had happened. That was Peter's last interaction with Jesus. Surely his denial must have felt like a huge burden to him. But that piece of unfinished business was so important that Jesus came back. Even though he had been killed, he came back. One morning he met Peter on the shore of the Sea of Galilee and asked him an all-important question. Inasmuch as Peter had denied Jesus three times it seems significant that Jesus asked Peter this question three times:

> "Peter, do you love me?"
> "Yes, Lord, you know I love you."
> "Peter, do you love me?"
> "Yes, Lord, you know I love you."
> "Peter, do you love me?"
> "Yes, Lord, you know I love you."
> "Then feed my sheep."

In that moment Jesus cleared the air between them, releasing Peter from his guilt and restoring their relationship. He was also telling Peter that he was suitable for future service, thus enabling Peter to move on. Life so often goes better when we speak openly to the fact that there is an elephant in the living room.

IV

HERE'S ANOTHER REASON people don't mention elephants in the living room. As long as we keep our observations to ourselves, it will seem to us that we have a firm hold on reality. If we don't mention aloud what we believe to be present, we can continue assuming that all relevant parties and all objective onlookers would agree as to the nature of the beast. The truth is that we soon tend to distort our unspoken hurts and grievances

When I lived in Indianapolis before moving to Bloomington—we lived in the Broad Ripple area—I enjoyed biking early in the morning several days a week and my route usually carried me straight north out College Avenue. Within two miles of home however there was a big, unchained dog that often lurked at the top of a steep hill. Just as I came to the top of this big hill, nearly exhausted, the large and vicious dog would come charging out of its front yard intending to attack me and I had to peddle as fast as I could to escape him. The hill was so steep and the dog was so big that biking was becoming less and less fun. Indeed I began biking less because of the beast.

One day as my wife and I were driving north on that same street, I said, "Now here's that big hill where the dog often waits for me up at the top." "What hill?," she asked. "This hill!," I answered. "This great big hill!" But now that my wife was along observing and rolling her eyes, it didn't look like much of a hill, but more like God's attempt at an incline. When we crested the incline I said, "Now there's where the dog often waits" and I pointed toward the white house with the red shutters. And there the beast was, out in the driveway, except that he wasn't huge any more but had somehow become a miniature schnauzer that looked as though he had been purchased because he was especially good with children. My wife said, "That's the beast?" I tried to recover by saying, "Well, when you're on a bike and are exhausted from this incline, he looks pretty big and vicious."

My point is this: if we dare to speak aloud about what is bothering us, everyone may not agree as to the size and shape of the beast. When we keep our grievances to ourselves, they tend to become inflated. Sometimes what we think is an elephant in our living room is a miniature schnauzer blown up.

V

THAT'S ENOUGH. Either you have already gotten my drift or you're not going to get it. My main point is that, whatever our reason for avoiding confrontation, we don't help our relationships by trying to sweep hurts, disappointments and grievances under the rug. The more we try to bury them, the bigger they get. The Bible says that we're not supposed to "let the sun go down on our anger." That means that our angers, hurts, grievances, and disappointments are meant to be expressed, not stuffed. Our anger isn't meant to be stored up or acted out. Our angers are meant to be listened to and acted upon. Likewise, our hurts, disappointments and grievances are meant to be listened to and acted upon. Hurts and disappointments are the soul's way of saying that it is time to speak up—time to work toward a more satisfying relationship—time to do something about the elephants that have found sanctuary in our living room.

Perhaps I can summarize all this with a few lines from the philosopher Gaston Bachelard, who had much influence in France earlier in this century. He said this:

> What is the source of our first suffering?
> It lies in the fact that we hesitated to speak.
> It was born in the moment when we accumulated silent
> things within us.

We increase the probability of hurting ourselves and others deeply when we allow our disappointments and complaints to accumulate. "Don't let the sun go down on your anger." We aren't doing anyone a favor if we wait months, years, or decades before we speak up. If we do speak up, we also need to be prepared to listen, for everyone may not agree with us about the size, shape, and origin of the beast. Still, it is important that we speak whenever what is not being said is getting between us and those we love.

August 1992

Thank God It's Summer

◆ ◆ ◆

Look at the birds of the air.
— Matthew 6:26a

S OMETIMES LABOR DAY arrives as a painful surprise. Those
are the years in which I have unconsciously plunged
through the summer like a CPA who thinks every month
is April or like an airliner on instruments hurtling through
clouds. When Labor Day came, announcing the end of those
summers, I felt that I had missed something. I *had* missed
something. I'd missed summer.

I suppose that missing one summer isn't a matter of life or
death—except that when we allow ourselves to miss one summer, we increase our chances of missing two summers or three
or four summers. And if we start missing summers, it won't be
long before we may miss a spring or a winter or a fall. And if we
miss whole seasons often enough, we may come to wonder
why our children who were kids just yesterday have so quickly
decided to go to college, to leave home, or to get married. In
extreme cases, not being able to enjoy summer may culminate
in not fully realizing that we have had a life. Today I want to
encourage you to pay attention to the fact that it is summer. On
one level that's all I want you to do. On another level I am trying
to subliminally trick you into paying attention to your life.

Hannah Gonen is a young Israeli woman who is the
central character in the novel *My Michael* by Amos Oz. She
wrote this in her journal one warm morning in July:

> Days pass without leaving a trace. I owe myself a solemn duty
> to record in this journal the passing of every day, every hour,
> for my days are mine . . . and they are flashing by like hills
> seen from the train on the way to Jerusalem.

I write in my own journal early most mornings, but I know that I cannot begin to record everything. I don't even try. Too much is flashing by. My goal is simply to be as present as possible wherever I am—to notice, smell, feel, hear, touch and taste whatever is going on around me. Right now, I am trying to notice that it is summer.

II

WHEN GOD WAS preparing to create Indiana and visited this portion of the Northwest Territory for the first time, God spent the night in the nearby town of Nashville at the Seasons Motel. It's hard to slip a good idea past God, and God said, "'Seasons', that sounds like a good idea—in Indiana I will have four of them. In autumn I will have the forests turn to brilliant colors so tourists will come, some plants will die, and the leaves will fall. Eventually the tourists will return home, and only natives will enjoy the intricate patterns etched against the sky by bare, black trees. Then I will do my underground work invisibly during the months I will call winter. In springtime buds will open and flowers will surface exuberantly, so people can see what I have been doing. And then between the urgent labors of seedtime and harvest, I will stretch summer. I will turn up the heat and humidity so human beings are not tempted to work as hard as usual. I'll make the sun rise earlier and the day linger longer. I'll invent swimming, and picnics, and girl's softball. I'll encourage children to play and adults to slow their pace. I'll invite humans to enjoy life more when it is summer."

The Bible claims that even God enjoys a change of pace. Genesis says:

> Thus the heavens and earth were finished, and all their multitude. And on the seventh day God finished the work that he had done, and he rested on the seventh day from all the work that he had done.

If God rests, how much more do human beings need to rest if they are to maintain their own inner harmony. In the Bible, rest is a blessing that the householder is meant to extend to all. One's self is to be given a rest; one's spouse and children are to be given a rest; one's animals are to be given a rest; one's workers are to be given a rest; and at stated intervals even one's land is to be given a rest. Work and rest are a rhythm that God has built into life. All creation needs a rest. One way for us to rest is to notice that it is summer.

III

REST ALONE MAY not restore us. Hans Selye, the Canadian physician and researcher who discovered the human stress response and pioneered stress management, liked to say that if all of us is tired we do need rest, but if only part of us is tired what we need is change—if only part of us is tired we need diversion. Many of us who spend so much of our lives indoors may be replenished by spending more time out-of-doors in the summer.

Have you ever noticed how often the New Testament portrays Jesus as being out-of-doors? He is seen on hillsides, along roads, beside lakes, on top of mountains, in village streets, and deep in desert wildernesses. Also notice that he speaks of birds, foxes, trees, fish, sheep, goats, camels, wheat, weeds, various kinds of soil, sand, rock, storms, floods, the color of the sky at dawn or in the evening and of the work that is necessary to maintain a farmer's fields.

It isn't that houses and other indoor spaces didn't exist in Jesus' time. Of course, they existed. Some people even had summer homes in the cooler mountain places. The prophet Amos is one who railed against rich persons who turned their backs on the poor while lounging in their summer homes on couches carved from ivory. No one ever accused Jesus of this. Jesus clearly rejected the soft and passive lifestyle of a first century couch potato. He lived most of his life being physically active outdoors, instead. The Bible also tells us that for renewal Jesus went out into nature early in the morning—he particularly liked "deserted places." Further, Jesus said things like

"Behold the birds of the air!" and "Consider the lilies of the field!" By so doing he was also asking his followers to pay attention to nature.

IV

I HAVE BEEN following Jesus' advice lately and I am finding that it replenishes me. My strategy is very simple. When weather permits I go out on the back porch in the morning for thirty minutes or more at five-thirty or six. Sometimes I pray, sometimes I read, sometimes I just sit. I also watch and listen to what is happening in nature—I admire the luxurious field of clover that had been my grass just a week before, I listen to the rat-a-tat-tat of a distant woodpecker digging bugs out of a dying tree, and I watch the band of crows circling above before they come in for a landing.

I have come to feel a lot better about crows simply by watching them. Last year at this time I still thought of a crow as being a feathered version of a junk yard dog. It annoyed me when the crows gobbled up the seed that we had scattered for chickadees, cardinals or Carolina wrens. I worried that they would bring down property values—having crows in the yard was like having grackles in the marten house. But lately I have been paying attention to them. I see now how cautious they are and how communal, warning one another and other animals whenever there seems to be danger. I see now that crows don't hang their heads or shuffle their feet, but are proud enough to hold up their heads and to march and even strut. More than two years ago my wife tried to explain to me that crows are beautiful, but I had been brainwashed by Yuppie birdwatchers to thrill only to warblers, towhees and grosbeaks and would have none of it. By paying attention in the early morning, I have gradually come to see that God made crows, as well as chickadees, and that crows are strong and graceful and beautiful—even elegant.

I have been watching hummingbirds, too. Until I came to Bloomington, I had seen a hummingbird only once and then I didn't really see it—all I knew was that something too big for a hornet was buzzing at the tip of my fishing pole—and then was gone before I could ask, "Was that a hummingbird?" Now hummingbirds are a common occurrence. Our feeder hangs from a tree, only a few feet away from where I sit examining the morning. A first there was only one. Now there are four or six. Some play and perch in the trees nearby. Others come bombing in from more than a hundred yards away. I don't know what it is about hummingbirds, but it is hard not to watch them and they are instruments of healing for me.

V

AT FIRST I JUST watched and enjoyed the morning. Now I am beginning to learn from it. I have learned, for instance, why Jesus so often spoke to his followers in nature-oriented parables. That's because it was through nature's parables that God spoke to him. When Jesus paid attention to nature with an open heart, God spoke to him. And if we pay attention to nature with an open heart, God will speak to us.

Take those hummingbirds, for example. They are teaching me about the foolishness of much human insecurity. Four hummingbirds can eat at our feeder at one time. By September they will learn to do that. But right now it is one bird feeding at a time. Right now there are spectacular air battles, as each bird tries to hoard all the nectar for itself. They hurl themselves at one another and sometimes collide. They do not understand that even if the feeder were to run dry, it would soon be replenished. They fret, worry and fight as though they are living in a world of scarcity. They can't see that there is nothing to worry about. It doesn't matter how many hummingbirds fly in to feed. Our love for them is trustworthy. The universe is abundant. God is good. They have found Fat City. As I watch them acting out their worry, they are teaching me how much easier it would be to share and to trust.

Sometimes I watch the squirrels. They are feeding on the last of the maple seeds now. They eat sitting on their haunches. Some have pure white bellies; others do not. But as they eat, they have one trait in common—they are attentive, they are watchful, they are wary. For good reason. If they are not watchful, they may be pounced upon by silent cats or yelping dogs. I ask God what the squirrels are saying to me. God answers, "There are dangers present in this life, and those who are wise remain vigilant."

More than a month ago a deer—a young doe—appeared at the edge of the woods. It was not grazing but was feeding on leaves at eye level and looked different than the rest. When the deer moved, I saw what the difference was. The doe's left front leg was broken. The lower leg was swinging free, as on a well-oiled hinge. The leg could bear no weight. The injury looked fresh—the deer was bewildered and in pain. Within myself I could feel the doe's pain and panic. I held my breath for the doe's sake, knowing that it was almost time for the neighbor's dogs to come sweeping through. There was no way that the deer would be able to run. But somehow it gathered itself and lurched and lunged back into the woods.

Later, it occurred to me that the doe could not have gone far. The ground is steep and uneven where she entered the woods. I feared that she would tumble into the deep ravine below—perhaps breaking another leg, being trapped there and starving to death. Without having any idea what I could do to help, I belatedly followed the deer into the woods. I searched for her for quite some time. I could not imagine her getting over the fallen logs on three legs, but she was gone. Still, through the pain spontaneously felt for her, God had sent me a message. God reminded me, in a deeply personal way, that all creatures on earth are brothers and sisters and that we are all a part of one large intricate web of life.

About noon yesterday, the deer which I assumed had died weeks ago reappeared at the very same spot. Her leg was still swinging free and she was still feeding at eye level, but she was moving more strongly now. The doe was crippled, but had made adjustments and had courageously managed to survive. This time the deer spoke to me not of the dangers we face or the pain we all know, but of the resiliency of life.

VI

SO THIS IS ONE of the ways that I am celebrating summer. Jesus said, "Behold the birds of the air!" and "Consider the lilies of the field!" and I am taking him literally. Because I am finding that sitting on the deck in the morning and paying attention to the natural world is so nourishing, I invite you to find your own way to notice that it is summer. Let us thank God that it is summer. Summer is a gift. Summer is a space God gives us to begin doing whatever will replenish our spirit.

June 1993

When Life Presents Us with Hills

◆　◆　◆

I lift up my eyes to the hills—
from whence will come my help?

— Psalm 121:1

OUR MINISTER TOLD this story when I was a boy. A preacher was stopped for speeding, and when the police officer came to the window of his car, he said, "I'm sorry, officer, I wasn't paying attention to my speed. I was thinking about last Sunday's sermon." The police officer was unmoved by this and said to the preacher, "You should have been thinking about next Sunday's."

That's one bit of advice that I take to heart. I have hardly left the church parking lot most Sundays, when I've already started to ask, "OK, God, what will WE talk about next week?" I'm supposed to get that question answered by Wednesday noon because that's when sermon titles are faxed into the newspaper. Last Wednesday morning I was out bicycling before breakfast, and I still didn't have a glimmer. I was off in the ozone somewhere reminding God of the deadline, and when I returned to normal consciousness and looked straight ahead, I saw a good-sized hill. And then I said, "That's it! I'll preach on the opening of the 121st Psalm: 'I lift up my eyes unto the hills. From whence cometh my help?'" So that's where today's sermon title, "When Life Presents Us with Hills," came from.

You may know that Bible scholars have differed over how that verse from the 121st Psalm should be translated. The King James Version, the Protestant standard for centuries, translated the verse as though the hills were a source of strength for the psalm writer: "I lift up my eyes unto the hills from whence cometh my help." That translation sparked centuries of sermons about how comforting and nourishing it is to take time to look up to the beauty, the majesty and the stability of God's hills. Most listeners nodded in agreement, having themselves often felt comforted, awed, and strengthened by the majesty of nature. However, the more technically correct translation is today believed to be the one that is published in the Revised Standard Version, which at the end of the second line adds a question mark. Then it reads: "I lift up my eyes unto the hills. From whence cometh my help?" Or as I have paraphrased it, "How am I going to get up this hill?" I reconcile the two versions by noticing that our impressions of hills often differ, depending upon the point from which we are viewing them. If I am in a valley looking up at a distant rim of hills I am likely to say, "Oh, look at those beautiful hills—their very presence strengthens me." But if I am at the bottom of a long, steep hill which I am soon going to have to climb, I am more likely to use the Revised Standard Version and say, "How am I going to get up this hill?" That's the version I'm using this morning, "How am I going to get up this hill?"

II

I HOPE YOU understand that I have been speaking on two levels. On one level I have been speaking about hills, and on the other level I have been speaking about "hills." The Bible does this all the time and Jesus, likewise, did it frequently. That is, on one level I am speaking literally about hills, and on another level I am speaking symbolically about hills. And while you may not have consciously recognized that I was speaking on two levels, your soul did realize that, and has already begun to think about the times in your life in which you have been called upon to climb challenging hills. Preaching looks like me talking to you, but that's the most superficial aspect of what's happening here. Actually, my soul is saying things to your soul, which at the level of consciousness we do not know are being said. So, too, your soul is speaking to my soul. And God is talking to your soul and my soul, so it is beneath the surface, at a much deeper level of communication, that what is most important is going on. That's why I like to say that preaching is really elevator music. It doesn't matter whether or not you listen to it. At a deeper level other more important ruminations and conversations are going on.

So, as I was saying, I was out on my bike about 6:30 the other morning and I came to this hill and I said maybe I can preach about hills. Maybe I can talk a little about what I've learned over the years about riding a bike up hills and while I'm doing that, maybe my soul and your soul could have a chat about life—about what's spiritually helpful when we suddenly look up in life and find that we have been presented with some rather challenging and even punishing hills.

III

I STARTED BIKING seriously about fifteen years ago when I was living in Indianapolis. The terrain there is relatively flat. When there was a hill it was short and I was younger then, so I'd just dig a little harder or stand up in the saddle and muscle my way up the hill. No problem. But after I'd been riding only a few months I took a trip with several of my ministerial colleagues from the far north side of Indianapolis to Bloomington for the United Methodist Annual Conference. The trip was about seventy miles—the farthest I'd ever ridden at that time—and the farther south we came the more clarity I gained over what is and isn't a hill. The most challenging hill on that trip—it doesn't seem nearly so formidable now—is south of Martinsville where Old 37 goes up toward Morgan-Monroe Park. True to form, when I saw the hill I started to muscle my way up the hill, and for the first quarter mile I left everyone else behind. But the hill didn't end. The hill went on and on, and soon I was exhausted and everyone whom I'd left behind was passing me.

Ninety-five-pound weaklings were passing me! Women minis-ters were passing me! I suddenly realized that I didn't know very much about how to climb when given long or steep hills. "How did you do that?" I later asked one of the riders who had pedaled past me. He said, "I never try to climb a big hill all at once. If I do, I get exhausted. So I climb the hill a little at a time. I look ahead maybe fifty feet until I see an unusual shadow on the road or a patch of sunlight. And I say, 'OK, I'm just going to ride from here to that patch of sunlight.' And when I get that far, I pick out another patch of sunlight or a crack in the road, and I say to myself, 'OK, now I'll just ride to that crack in the road.'" He said, "When I am faced with a really challenging hill, I just climb it a little bit at a time."

A few years afterwards, I rode with four friends from Indi-anapolis to Gatlinburg, Tennessee, and then another day up into the Smoky Mountains, and on that trip I learned some more about climbing hills. From Indianapolis to Berea, Ken-tucky, the hills tended to be mostly rolling and manageable. But on the afternoon of the third day when we were south of Berea, something new happened as we approached a hill. On the right-hand side an extra lane of highway appeared. If you are ever riding your bike and another lane appears, take note of it. That is not a bike path built for your safety and convenience at taxpayers' expense. Rather, that is a sign. The road is widen-ing for a reason. God is trying to tell you something. That lane is for trucks which will be slowed to a crawl by what is up ahead. When life gets that steep and the climb is that long, all the rules change. Suddenly, the name of the game is "Take care of yourself." Suddenly, the name of the game is "Survival." It was on such hills that I learned that when our life path is so steep and so challenging that it's painful, it's time to join the slow vehicles in the right-hand lane, time to get down into the lowest gear you have, to proceed as slowly as you can, to tell yourself that eventually this, too, will pass, to just grind it out, and to do your very best to endure. I have friends who like to talk to themselves when laboring through such a climb. Re-

membering a childhood bedtime story, they chant to themselves, "I think I can, I think I can, I think I can." Personally, I
find it more helpful to be honest with myself and with God. So,
I keep saying, "I wish I weren't, I wish I weren't, I wish I
weren't." Why pretend that a punishing climb was in your life
plan? But when I get to the top, no matter how tired I am, I
shift to, "I'm glad I did, I'm glad I did, I'm glad I did!"

I remember one long, steep hill in the Smokies on which I
utilized all I had learned. I rode from this crack to that patch of
sunlight, and from this patch of sunlight to that sign by the
side of the road, and I got down into my lowest gear, and rode
as slowly as I could, and just tried to survive, but this particular
hill kept climbing for several miles. Finally, I was so exhausted
and my body was protesting to such a degree that I said, "If I try
to ride to one more patch of sunlight, I am going to die." It was
then that I discovered another creative strategy for making it
over the steepest hills of life. Instead of dying, I stopped to rest.
When I'd rested sufficiently I went on and finished the climb.
It's true what the Bible says, "Those who wait for the Lord shall
renew their strength, they shall rise up on wings like eagles,
they shall walk and not faint, they shall run and not be weary."
If you are laboring through hill country and think you can't go
on, you don't have to die—instead, find ways to rest—find
times to wait—until you are able to go on.

IV

THAT'S MOST OF what I know about hill climbing. Take the long
ones a little at a time, take the most punishing ones in your
lowest gear as slowly as you can and, if the climb seems beyond
your strength, don't be afraid to give yourself a rest. But there is
one more technique I have learned. When your mind and
body and spirit are tired and there is still a climb ahead of you,
it is possible to strengthen yourself with invisible resources.

On that first bike trip from Indianapolis to Bloomington
some years ago, I'd almost made it. I took a rest at Musgrave's

Orchard, and then I had only a few more miles to go. That's a pretty section of the ride, and there are some fun downhills, and before long I had only one more hill to go—the one that goes up to the Fire House on Old 37 north of town. I rode up that hill in a Jeep a few weeks ago and was amused by how small a hill it really is. But on that hot summer day when I was climbing it for the first time and had almost seventy miles behind me, I didn't think I'd be able to continue. Just then I looked up to the top of the hill, and I saw a friend of mine standing there with a camera. Louie Cain had driven his car down with us in case of emergency, and there he was waiting to take my picture as I climbed up the last hill. That renewed a little bit of my strength. I said to myself, "Louie's up there—I can't fall off my bike now." And with that as encouragement, I finished the climb. But when I made it to the top, Louie wasn't there. He'd never been there. In my fatigue, I had imagined him.

That's when I learned that I can be strengthened for the more difficult times of life by imagining myself being in the presence of people who are not physically or tangibly there. Sometimes, when life gets especially difficult, I talk to my father who died several years ago; or I imagine that my Grandfather Seidel, whom I loved so dearly as a boy, is still standing by; or that my children are in the wings pulling for me. I imagine them saying, "Don't quit now, son. Don't lose hope, Dad. Hang in there, Dave! We know you can; we know you can," and somehow their invisible presence strengthens me. Remembering those who care about you—whether or not they are visibly present— whether they are living or dead—will also strengthen you when your mind, body and spirit are tired and the climb is still long.

The question isn't really, "Do we want hills in our life?" but rather "How will we approach them when they are inescapably there?" At such times, the methods we choose will matter.

June 1994

Ghosts

◆　◆　◆

... since we are surrounded by so great
a cloud of witnesses ...

—Hebrews 12:1

PHYSICISTS IN THE 1920s couldn't make their equations about electrons come out right. They could accurately describe a single electron but could not describe what was going on between electrons. That was because each electron is surrounded by a cloud of other, ghost-like particles, which fleetingly come and go. In reality, there are no isolated electrons. Quantum ghosts are everywhere, forming a cloud around each electron. It was these ghosts that were contradicting the equations.

As a young physicist, unfettered by tradition, Richard Feynman suggested that scientists not look at isolated electrons, but that they always look at the electron plus the cloud of ghosts that surrounded it. That led to an immediate breakthrough. When the electron's ghosts were seen to be a part of its identity and makeup, the theoretical formulas worked. The electrons became more predictable.

II

WHEN I LEARNED about electron "ghosts" several months ago, I immediately began to apply the concept to human beings. It occurred to me, for instance, that I have "ghosts" that come and go—experiences out of my past, certain persons out of my past, a flurry of messages out of my past, specific hurts or fears from out of the past, dreams, and disappointments from out of my past—that may not be haunting me in every moment, but do still come and go. I thought that perhaps this is what we mean by the subconscious—the abyss into which our ghosts go and from which they return uninvited, when certain situations or events appeal to them. I recall a time ten years ago when I was standing in the checkout line in a super market. Admittedly, I was harried and tired and it had been a long day, but I still possessed my equilibrium until in the express lane next to me, two young men with a half-full shopping cart rudely pushed ahead of an older couple who had been waiting for some time. You might think that this was really none of my business—after all, the elderly couple did nothing to assert themselves and I was not delayed in any way—but I found myself furious and seething within. A ghost from my childhood—the ghost of Batman, Captain Marvel or the Green Hornet—some fighter for justice who took up residence inside me years earlier while I was reading comic books or listening to adventure stories on the radio after school on a dark winter's afternoon—some boyhood crime fighter—came unsummoned from out of the deeps and took possession of my body, until I saw that my hand was shaking and was pointing to the two rude young men, and I heard myself screaming to their cashier, "They have more than twelve items!" When everyone turned to see whose scream had violated the agreed upon civility of the supermarket, the ghosts quickly returned to the deeps, leaving me to face the staring crowds alone.

In that moment I better understood the words of Nikos Kazantzakis, who in *Saviors of God* wrote of such experiences:

> You are not one; you are a body of troops. The race of people from which you come is the huge body of the past, the present, and the future.
>
> You are not free. Myriad invisible hands hold your hands and direct them. When you rise in anger, a great-grandfather froths at your mouth; when you make love, an ancestral caveman growls with lust; when you sleep, tombs open in your memory till your skull brims with ghosts.

"No, we have not gone," the dead cry out. "We have not detached ourselves from you. Deep in your entrails we continue the struggle. Deliver us."

Is it possible that human beings as well as electrons are surrounded by a cloud of ghosts—that you and I are somewhat unpredictable even to ourselves, because of shadows out of the past that come and go? Is that why the equations don't work—is that why we don't do the things that we want to do but do some of the things that we don't want to do? Is that why child abuse is so often a family tradition? Why Serbs and Bosnians and Croats can't get along? Is that why it is sometimes hard to love another? Is that why we can be crippled by curses spoken to us decades ago? Why we are afraid to take certain risks? Why divorces are so hard to transcend? Is it possible that you and I are never isolated and alone, but that we are interacting with an invisible cloud of ghosts? That's my experience. You won't know me until you know my ghosts. I won't understand you, until I understand your ghosts. Therefore, in many ways human beings will remain mysteries to one another. When Flip Wilson used to say, "The devil made me do it!," he was talking about his ghosts. When we act in ways that puzzle us or seem, to those who know us best, not to be like us at all, we are apt to be influenced by ghosts. When we violate our own cherished values; when we injure a loved one or become harmful to ourselves . . . ghosts! We are not entirely free. We are constantly interacting with a cloud of persons, experiences, messages, hurts and memories from out of the past. They come and go. When our spirits our weak, the past can take possession of us.

III

INTERESTINGLY, THE BIBLICAL answer is not to try to get rid of the ghosts. Jesus warned of the dangers when a house or a person has lost all its ghosts. Empty spaces can be filled with demons worse than before, he said. Besides, if we try to rid ourselves of our ancestors they are not likely to go. If we try to ignore old hurts, they will only bury themselves and fester more deeply within us. If we pretend that there are no ferocious, greedy, lustful, angry and violent ancestors within us, we may be shocked by the power with which they overtake us in an hour of spiritual weakness.

The biblical answer is not to deny the ghosts, but to acknowledge them and then surround ourselves with another kind of cloud—a cloud of what the Bible calls "witnesses." Witnesses are examples of faith. We help to make ourselves spiritually strong—we become less susceptible to ghosts—when we surround ourselves with vivid examples of faith.

That's what is going on in the Letter to the Hebrews. That author is reminding the Hebrew people of the many faithful examples in their past: Abraham, Moses, Noah, Sarah, Deborah, Barak and many more. These heroic figures are not gone. They still swirl around and within us. They strengthen and protect us when we pay attention to them, but only when we pay attention to them.

For myself, I find it helpful to become conscious of those who are witnesses for me. Those whose example can help to guide my life. Those whose way nourishes my spirit. I think of my father and his attempts to share with me his own simple faith. I remember my grandfather, who was both strong and kind. I recall certain teachers who believed in me before I believed in myself. I think of those who were giants of faith for me: Martin Luther King, Jr., Dom Helder Camara of Brazil, and Archbishop Oscar Romero of El Salvador. I recall the spirited Teresa of Avila, who revitalized the Church in Spain in the six-teenth century, and St. Bruno, who built his hermitage atop the craggiest mountain. I remember theologians like Paul Tillich and Dietrich Bonhoeffer, who articulated the Christian faith in ways that helped me to believe. I remember friends along life's way who helped me to know—even in times of great failure and difficulty—that I was of value and worth and that I was loved. I recall authors, artists, and musicians who have opened my heart to more and more life. Each of us would do well to surround ourselves with those who are vibrant examples of faith for us. To immerse ourselves in their witness.

IV

As TODAY WE prepare to share in the Sacrament of Holy Communion, I would remind us that a part of what we are meant to feed upon here is the community of faith. On one level that means allowing ourselves to be strengthened by the presence of those who are sitting or kneeling beside us. On another level that means feeding on the witness and example of all faithful souls living and dead, Jesus Christ being the chief cornerstone. We will always be vulnerable to ghosts—to hurtful persons, messages or experiences out of the past—especially in careless moments or when our spirits are wounded or weak. Nevertheless, if we consciously surround ourselves with a cloud of witnesses—if we live day-by-day in the awareness of those who exemplify faith for us—they will strengthen and protect us. As we kneel this morning, let us remember those whose lives can help to make us strong. In our hearts, let us feed on their examples, by faith with thanksgiving.

September 1993

All Things Are Possible

◆　◆　◆

Jesus said to him, "All things are possible to
him who believes."

— Mark 9:23

J ESUS WAS HAVING a bad day. He had just come down from the
mountaintop where he had been with Peter, James and
John. That had been a very special time away. Moses and
Elijah—patron saints of Israel who in former times had epito-
mized the Law and the Prophets—had spoken to him there.
The disciples had been awestruck by Jesus' appearance on the
mountain. The Bible says that Jesus had been "transfigured"
before them—his clothes becoming a glistening, radiant white.
Also, God had come down to them and they had all heard
God's voice from out of the cloud, saying, "This is my beloved
Son; listen to him." That was a high point of Jesus' ministry,
but when he came down from the mountain he had some
difficulty reentering his everyday life.

You know what that's like, don't you? On a get-away-
weekend, you have fun and relax and may even feel that you
have your life in a new and more manageable state. But then
you return and life is just as chaotic as before. Maybe the phone
is ringing as you walk in the door: "Can you come to work right
now?," the panicked voice asks. "There is a crisis at the office."
Or upon reentry your four year-old twins are screaming and
the baby is sick. Or lightning has split your favorite back yard
oak tree, a huge limb has fallen on the car and your basement
is flooded. You know what sometimes happens upon reentry—you know what I mean.

When Jesus returned to sea level, the scribes and his disciples were arguing and squabbling—just like before. The crowds were milling around and waiting for him—just like before. The disciples had been helpless in the face of a boy with a demon—just like before. And the father of a sick boy was pleading with Jesus for help—just like before. His enemies were on the edge of the crowd watching and waiting for him to make a slip—just like before. In the face of all that familiar activity, Jesus' getaway weekend evaporated in an instant. Suddenly it felt as though he had never been away and Jesus said to them all:

> You faithless generation; how long must I be with you; how long must I put up with you?

The disciples who had been waiting for Jesus to come back from the mountain must have felt sharply the sting of his words. For they had tried to do what Jesus himself might have done had he been there, but were powerless to emulate him. They had wanted to help the boy and his father, but had been unable to heal.

II

I CAN SYMPATHIZE with those disciples. I remember the first time I truly tried to heal. I was a student minister many years ago in Milwaukee's inner-city. A young boy in our neighborhood was taken to the hospital with a life-threatening illness. The boy came from a family that was both large and poor. The many children lived amidst increasing tension between their father and mother who openly and loudly threatened each other with divorce. The boy who was four years old had been feverish and in great pain for several days. In the midst of the usual uproar no one had put the seriousness of the symptoms together until it was too late. It may be that from the very beginning it had been too late. As it was, the boy was in a coma when he reached the hospital and despite eight days of intensive care, he died. We buried him on a bitterly cold day in a cemetery far from his neighborhood. Peter's grave was dug right beside the cemetery's tractor shed.

That was the first time I was exposed to a child dying. I found myself going to the hospital twice a day—I went in the morning and I went at night. I prayed for him. I hurt for him. I wanted to heal. It wasn't just the disease. Ninety-nine percent of me knew that the outcome of his illness was out of my hands. But there was also all the pain of the boy's family; the bewilderment of his brothers and sisters; the guilt of his mother and father—the way they blamed each other and failed to help each other. I didn't expect to cast out such demons quickly. I knew that healing would take time. But a few days after the funeral their house was empty when I called. A neighbor reported that the father had walked out abruptly and that the next day the mother and children had also disappeared. It wasn't just the disease. It was also the boy's family. I wanted to help; I wanted to heal; but I could not. I can sympathize with the disciples who found themselves powerless in the face of a convulsing boy.

III

"Bring the boy to me," Jesus said. When they did, immediately the boy fell into a convulsion, foaming at the mouth and rolling on the ground. "How long has he had this?" Jesus asked.

"From childhood," the father said. "But if you can do anything, have pity on us and help us."

"If I can!" Jesus exploded. "All things are possible to him who believes!"

"I believe! I believe!" answered the father. "Help my unbelief. Please. Help my unbelief."

When I was three years old my mother was shocked to find that there was a strange bulge visible in my abdomen when I was stretched flat. It proved to be a large growth pushing forward from my spine against my internal organs. A team of specialists was gathered to perform exploratory surgery. They opened me up, poked around, consulted with one another and said, "There's nothing we can do; sew him up." The specialists left. Our family doctor—the physician who had delivered me and had called his colleagues to help him—decided to stay. He cut at the growth. He wasn't certain that what he was doing would help me, but he installed some tubing inside the cut, creating a drain. Then he sewed me up. He told my parents that I would probably live only a few months. Sitting on the steps of the hospital, he asked them to pray. But the crude drain worked and within a year the growth had gone away. I am still here, in part, because Gilbert Mueller, M.D.—general practitioner and surgeon—chose not to surrender too soon. Instead, he chose to risk one more failure and one more disappointment. He chose to believe, if only in part, that healing was possible. Does that mean that every time someone believes that healing is possible, sickness will go away? No, that simply means that healing happens most frequently through those who believe that healing is possible.

Here's a very different example. Early one morning last week, Boris Yeltsin, the president of Russia, received word at his home that a coup had begun and that Mikhail Gorbachev was under house arrest in his dacha on the Black Sea. Yeltsin hurried to his office in Moscow minutes before KGB officers were able to detain him. There he learned more about the coup—that those seeking to take over the government were backed by the military, the powerful Interior Ministry and the KGB. They had troops and tanks and had taken control of the media. I don't know how he would have talked about his decision, but Boris Yeltsin was faced with a theological question: Was his presidency already lost or might the coup be turned back, if only he believed? As you know, he chose to believe; he stood up, personally opposing the coup, calling for help from the people, issuing decrees. Was it certain that he would succeed? Absolutely not. He himself might have been captured or killed. Afraid, the people might have stayed home. Unconcerned for world opinion, those who controlled the tanks might have crushed the protesters, reenacting Tiananmen Square. Does that mean that our hopes will be fulfilled, if only we believe? No, that simply means that victory most frequently happens through those who have the faith and the courage to believe that victory is possible. Not certain, but possible.

One must ask whether healing can enter any situation unless someone within that situation dares to hope, risk, trust and believe. How, for example, will love ever reenter a strained and shattered marriage, unless the persons within that marriage dare to hope, risk, trust and believe? How will an emotionally troubled, or mentally retarded or physically handicapped child be helped to seize her fullest potential, unless someone close to that child dares to hope, risk, trust and believe? How will the evil spirits of injustice or bigotry or fear or violence be driven from our individual lives or from our society, unless someone dares to hope, risk, trust and believe? I am not saying that trust and faith alone will suffice to heal. I am simply raising the question that Jesus is raising: Do we not lessen our power to heal the moment we stop believing that healing is possible?

IV

WHILE JESUS SAID, "All things are possible to him who believes," that was not, in fact, the way he found life to be in many instances. Yes, all things were possible, but everything he wanted did not happen. Not even for Jesus. Not everything he longed and labored and prayed for came to pass. "All things are possible" was his faith. That was not always his experience.

Within the New Testament it is clear that at times Jesus was disappointed and frustrated. The behavior of his own disciples reminded him that it was a faithless generation. He could not bring that whole generation into God's Kingdom, no matter how hard he tried. "All things are possible to him who believes," said Jesus, but he himself could not make even his closest disciples understand. He came to open people's eyes that they might see the truth, and yet many did not like his truth and schemed and plotted against him. He came that people might deeply understand the meaning of God's Law, and yet so many saw him as a destroyer of that Law. When Jesus said, "All things are possible to him who believes," he was talking about his faith—he was talking about the way in which he chose to face the world. "All things are possible" was his hope; that was not at all times his experience. Jesus preferred the hurt and disappointment that sometimes comes to those who believe, rather than the internal death of those who no longer believe that victory is possible. When we believe that all things are possible, we increase our vulnerability to disappointment and we also increase our power to heal.

V

THREE OR FOUR years ago—maybe five—on a Friday afternoon I was making calls at St. Vincent's Hospital in Indianapolis. In the hospital's computer, I discovered the name of one of our congregation's children—a four-year-old boy—and I added him to my list of persons to visit.

When I went to his room, the door was ajar slightly. It was mostly dark inside. Hearing voices, I hesitated outside the door. The doctor was talking to the boy's parents, and I heard enough to piece the situation together. The boy—who had had a brain growth at birth—had been healthy for his short four years. But recently he had begun to complain of headaches and had grown more and more listless. One week of tests at another hospital had produced no diagnosis. Another week at this hospital had likewise left the physicians stumped. "If he is not improved by Monday," I heard the doctor say, "we will have to do exploratory brain surgery." The doctor left the room and I went in. Both the boy's mother and father were there. The lad himself was not comatose but looked very ill and was deathly still. I talked with his parents a while and before leaving I asked them if they would pray with me for their son. They said, "Yes." I took the mother's hand and she took the hand of her husband who was standing on the other side of the bed. I was about to take the boy's limp hand, but a quiet voice inside me said, "Place your hand on his head." I did and we began to pray. I have no idea what I said. What happened next was subtle—something that I had never experienced before and I have not experienced again. As we prayed together I felt energy coming out of my hand. When I left I had the feeling that something had happened. "It's possible that he's going to get better," I said to myself alone.

I was away that weekend. When I returned on Monday, the door to the boy's room was open and the lights were on. The boy was sitting up, laughing, as he watched cartoons on television. His mother was packing his things. "We're going home," she said. "Almost immediately after we prayed on Friday, our son began to get better," she reported. "He kept getting better until Saturday afternoon and then he started to slip back. So we called two friends and they joined us here and we prayed again. And our son got better again and now is back to normal. A few minutes ago the doctor discharged him." "I knew it!," I said to myself. "I knew it!" On Friday I had felt energy going into him.

VI

WHAT THEN SHALL we make of these things?

Last week I was again in Indianapolis—this time to visit one of our members who was hospitalized there. On the way I stopped at another hospital to see an old friend. Our friendship goes back twenty years. By all appearances she is slowly dying. As our visit drew to a close, she took my hand and said, "Pray for me." I did. I don't recall what I said. I did notice that no special energy flowed out of my hand, but that energy—at the very least some human warmth and encouragement—did seem to come to me from her hand. Did our praying help her? I don't know. While all things are possible, in this world nothing is certain, even when we believe. Not even Jesus had everything turn out his way. Nevertheless, when we are faithful, the mere fact that healing is possible is sufficient reason to hope, pray, risk, care and touch, and believe.

August 1991

O For a Thousand Ears to Hear

◆　◆　◆

Now there are varieties of gifts, but the same Spirit.

— I Corinthians 12:4

RECENTLY, I HAD what some people call an "Aha" experience. If that language doesn't speak to you, let me say instead that a light went on upstairs. That is to say, the truth clattered down. I had an insight. If I wanted to share what happened with a particular kind of religious audience, instead of saying that I had an "Aha" experience, I might witness to the fact that the Holy Spirit caused the scales to fall from my eyes or tell them how Jesus touched my eyes that I might more clearly see. To a group of humanists I might say that because of something I read, an old and seemingly outmoded religious concept was creatively reframed for me.

If you speak only one of these languages, by now you are probably confused. However, if you are multilingual, you know that I have been saying the same thing several ways. I have been saying (this is the eighth version) that I recently came to see something differently—not as the result of a long period of study, research or reflection, but in a sudden, unexpected moment of illumination.

II

HERE'S WHAT TRIGGERED the insight. In *The Way of the Dream* I was reading one of the conversations between Fraser Boa and Marie-Louise von Franz. They had been talking about the role of angels in ancient scriptures and when Fraser Boa asked Marie-Louise von Franz where she saw angels today, she answered like this:

Well, I can tell you what happened to my friend, Miss Hannah. We were driving into town and suddenly she stepped on the brakes so hard that I flew into the window. When I looked up there was nothing in front of us. At that moment a child jumped out from behind a parked car and ran right in front of our car. But we had already stopped. I said to Miss Hannah, "How on earth did you do that? The child wasn't visible when you stopped. It wasn't yet visible at all." And she said, "Something in me told me, 'Brake at once, brake at once.' I don't know what that was." Now, ancient man would have said, "My guardian angel told me that." It was as if a benevolent presence had interfered. Miss Hannah had no idea why she braked. She just felt as if a voice in her car was saying, "Brake! Brake!" and she did.

That's what triggered my "Aha" experience. I mean, that's when the Holy Spirit caused the scales to drop from my eyes. That's when I saw that one person's hunch can be another person's heavenly host.

III

I AM NOT comfortable when people talk about angels. Neurologically speaking, angels cross my wires. In part, it's because I am a Protestant Christian who was born in the twentieth century. In America, no less. In my neighborhood the Catholic kids talked about angels all the time, but nobody expected a Methodist kid to talk like that. I attended worship from an early age. People thought I wasn't listening while I was scribbling in the bulletin with my father's Eversharp pencil, but I was. And there I learned that we Methodists do not need (or even want) intermediaries between ourselves and God. We don't need priests, and saints, and angels—I'm speaking of my own spiritual upbringing now—my own long held biases. And then I went off to college to study aeronautical engineering and I wouldn't have graduated yet if I'd insisted on talking about the flight characteristics of angels. In those days they had a room for people of that persuasion at the Student Health Center. So don't expect to see me loitering in the angel section of any local bookstores or watching a Geraldo "Heavenly Beings I've Known" special on TV. When talk about angels comes up, my wires cross and spark and give off smoke—my brain just doesn't get it. But when I read the story of Miss Hannah braking before the child ran into the street, I began to see.

I had an experience like that once. It was a Maundy Thursday evening twenty years ago. It was dark and raining slush and sleet. I was backing out of my driveway near the end of a dead-end street. The radio was playing loudly. As I started backing up, I thought I heard someone screaming above the noise of the radio, "Stop! Stop! Help me. Stop! Help me!" I stopped, turned off the radio, rolled down the window and listened. Nothing. No sound, apart from the hissing of the falling sleet. I started up again. "Stop! Stop! Help me. Stop! Help me!" I stopped and rolled down the window again. Nothing but the sound of sleet. But it was too eerie. So I got out of the car. Twenty-five feet behind me, an elderly neighbor was lying in her bathrobe face down in the street. She had slipped and fallen on the ice when taking her trash out. No one else was outside. Only this woman. And she was unconscious. She was not the one who had been calling to me. How do I explain what happened? Being who I am, I don't. For me it is an inexplicable mystery. Like Miss Hannah, I simply know that I heard a voice. "Something" told me to stop. I seem to have been guided by an intelligence greater than my own. I might call that intelligence "intuition" or "God" or "the uncon-scious" or "ESP." I don't know quite what to call that intelli-gence. I have friends who might say that I was warned by spirit guides from another astral plane. I don't know what it was. But the next time I hear someone talk about their encounter with an angel, I'm going to listen as hard as I can to determine whether they might be talking about a situation similar to the one that happened to Miss Hannah or to me. Rather than rejecting their language, I'm going to try to translate those sounds into a language that makes sense to me.

IV

THIS ISN'T A sermon about angels. It's really a sermon about the need in today's church and world for people who can hear in more than one language. The most Methodist of Methodist hymns for the past two hundred years has been Charles Wesley's hymn "O For a Thousand Tongues to Sing My Great Redeemer's Praise." The prayer implicit in that hymn is that we would learn to speak in many languages, so that we would be able to express the love of God to people who hear in differing ways. That's an old Methodist rule of thumb. John Wesley insisted that the Gospel was always meant to be put in the language of the people. I have long felt the importance of that and when I am teaching or preaching I try to consider who is in the room. Is this an audience that would better understand me if I said, "Then the Holy Spirit caused the scales to drop from my eyes" or is this an audience that could more easily relate to "Then I had an unexpected insight." I think it's always important to take pains to express our message in a way that increases the likelihood that it will be understood. Even in our personal relationships.

I remember a friend of mine who years ago was having a hard time expressing to his wife the love he had for her. He was trying to tell her, but the language he was using wasn't getting the job done. Holidays like Christmas, and birthdays and anniversaries were important to her, but they weren't important to him, and he often forgot them. Every time he forgot such a day, she felt less loved. Then one Christmas he planned well ahead. He was proud of remembering and of going out shopping by himself to find the gift. But, he later reported that when she opened the gift, she felt even less loved than before.

"Why?", I asked. "I don't know," he said. He had obeyed the Golden Rule. He had done unto her as he would have liked her to have done unto him. He loved her and was concerned for her safety and well-being, so as the first Christmas gift he had purchased in years, he bought snow tires for her car. Knowing them both, my heart sank at the pain both of them experienced around that gift. I understood the wife's desire that her husband express his love to her in a language that she could more easily understand. I always think its important for us to try to do that. But in a world where people speak in so many different languages, I'm wondering if it isn't equally important to pray for a Thousand Ears with Which to Hear. I can understand the pain my friend's wife felt when she opened her Christmas gift and it was snow tires. But what a blessing it would have been for both of them, if by some sort of miracle, she could have received the clumsy gift in the way her husband had intended and, therefore, sensed within it his care, his concern for her well-being, and his love.

V

IN CHRISTIAN TRADITION the weeks after Christmas—the weeks of Epiphany—have long emphasized speaking in a variety of tongues—that is, speaking of God's love in a way that crosses the barriers of culture and language that so often divide. Where that leads, if we aren't careful, is to pouring all our energies into getting other people to hear us. Pollsters, politicians, public relations experts and spin doctors have perfected the art of speaking to people in their own language, whether they are speaking the truth or not. But where are the people who are struggling to hear what others are saying in strange tongues? Where are the adults who are trying to listen to teens in their language? Where are the men who want to hear what women are saying? Where are the women who are struggling to hear what men can't quite say in women's language? Where are the rich who want to hear with new ears the despair or anger of the poor? Where are the religious who want to hear from seemingly secular persons who experience spirit in non-traditional ways? Where are the fundamentalists who want to better understand non-fundamentalists? Where are the non-fundamentalists willing to listen to fundamentalists for the divine realities that may lie beneath both their languages? Where are those who are not only concerned to speak across barriers that divide, but are working to hear across barriers that divide?

When God's Spirit fell upon the early church at Pentecost, the Bible doesn't say that people were able to speak in different languages, which is the way that passage is usually interpreted. Instead, the Bible says that those upon whom the Spirit fell were able to hear strange languages as though they were their own. In times past, being able to speak in strange tongues was considered a highly prized spiritual gift. Today a willingness to listen to languages other than one's own would seem an even more important gift.

January 1995

Had Jesus Lived a Hundred Years

◆　◆　◆

And taking the twelve, he said to them,
"Behold, we are going up to Jerusalem,
and everything that is written of the Son of man
by the prophets will be accomplished."

— Luke 18:31

ONCE ATTENDED A life planning workshop in which two questions were asked. The first question was, "If you knew you had only six months to live, how would you spend your time?" Second, "What would you do if you knew you had a hundred more years to live?"

I find those to be two very different questions. At least I find my answers moving in two different directions. If I had only six more months to live I think I'd probably begin by cleaning out my garage and my office so no one else would have to do it. I'd certainly make use of however many vacation days I had accrued. And I'd spend as much time as I could with family and friends. If, on the other hand, I knew that I had a hundred more years to go, I think I'd go back and actually read Plato and Shakespeare; I'd try once again to master Spanish; I'd finally learn to type with more than two fingers; and I would more aggressively explore the possibilities that are inherent within compound interest. I find that when I think short-term I tend to ask, "What do I want to do now?" and when I think long-term I tend to ask, "What, in the end, will I wish I had done?" For me, those are often two very different questions.

II

IN TODAY'S GOSPEL lesson Jesus is looking only a short distance ahead—roughly sixty miles and a few weeks. He is going to Jerusalem for Passover and expects to die there. Indeed, throughout his three years of ministry he seems to have lived with an unusually short time horizon—"Verily, verily I say unto you, the time is coming and now is" and again "The time is fulfilled, and the Kingdom of God has come near; repent." The Gospels present Jesus' ministry as fast-paced. Mark frequently uses the word "immediately"—"Immediately he called them," and "Immediately they left their nets," and "Immediately he made the disciples get into the boat." Mark also uses transition phrases such as "after this," and "as soon as they left the synagogue," and "that evening," and "in the morning," and "after a few days." Events take place one after another, with little space between them. Moreover, history is seen as about to go into a skid. The end is near. There is no time or need to think about pension plans or compound interest. Jesus is on the brink. Those who walk behind him are marching toward the end of history, even as he is striding toward his death.

It occurred to me recently that this short time horizon undoubtedly had a strong influence on the teachings of Jesus. Is it possible that some of his teachings are best understood as being most appropriate when time is short?

> • Therefore I tell you . . . take no thought for tomorrow . . . do not worry about your life . . . what you shall eat, or what you shall drink, or what you shall put on . . .

> • If a Roman soldier says to you "Walk with me a mile" . . . Hey, that won't last much longer—walk with him two miles. If someone tries to steal your coat, give him your cloak as well . . .

> • Don't lay up treasures on earth. . . . The time is short—lay up treasures in heaven . . .

• I'm sending you out two by two. When you get to a town and they listen to you, stay a while. If they don't listen to you, don't waste your time—shake the dust of that town from your feet—move on as quickly as you can—get out of there!

Was it this sense of extreme urgency that caused Jesus to heal wherever and whenever he was—while he was visiting a synagogue or passing through a town, even though it was the Sabbath? Was it his sense of urgency that caused Jesus to teach his disciples to pray, "Give us today's allotment of bread?" Is that why he made a bold symbolic statement when he entered the Temple—overthrowing a few tables—a strategy that certainly upset things for an hour or two, but ultimately had no chance for success? Is that the way Jesus would have tried to change things, if he had expected to live a hundred years?

Jesus must be understood as a man with a very short time horizon—as a man with an unusual sense of urgency.

III

THERE IS AN interesting contrast in the life of the Hebrew prophet Jeremiah. Actually, there were many religious figures in Israel's history with a heightened sense of urgency who warned of dangers that were coming. "Can't you see what's happening?" they asked. "Wake up before it's too late!" In his youth Jeremiah, too, proclaimed that urgent message, warning of wars that were to come. In his later years, however, Jeremiah's message changed from one of urgency to one of patience—not because Jeremiah himself had changed, but because Israel's situation had changed.

Indeed, the war Jeremiah predicted years earlier finally came. Jerusalem was defeated in war by King Nebuchadnezzar, and many of her people were carried off into exile in Babylon. Suddenly the people became impatient. "You're a prophet," they said to Jeremiah. "Talk to God. Get us out of this." "That's not the way it is going to be," Jeremiah said. "I have talked to God, and God says you're going to be in Babylon for a long time. True, there are other prophets saying that deliverance will come soon, but they are wrong. They are telling you what you want to hear. The truth is that you will be in Babylon for at least seventy years." And because they were in a long-term situation, here is the un-Jesus-like advice that God gave to the people through Jeremiah:

• Build houses and live in them.

• Plant gardens and eat what they produce.

• Take wives and have sons and daughters.

• Take wives for your sons and give your daughters in marriage.

• Multiply while you are in exile. Do not let your numbers decrease.

• Seek the welfare of Babylon because that is where you are now living. Pray for Babylon, because that is where you are now living. Your well-being and the city of Babylon are now linked.

Interesting advice. Un-Jesus-like advice. Apparently, one God-message does not fit every situation. Before God speaks to people, God bothers to notice what time it is.

IV

BECAUSE HE DIED young—and because he lived such an urgent life—there were many life issues that Jesus did not face.

He did not have to balance family life with his work life. He was single-minded and intense, living mostly on the road, and therefore could unashamedly tell Martha that she spent too much time in the kitchen. There is no biblical evidence to suggest that Jesus spent any time in the kitchen—that it was ever necessary for Jesus to take time out to do his laundry or wash dishes. Others, like Martha, seem to have taken care of those things for him. He didn't have to worry about how to care for his mother, Mary, in her old age. He was never pulled between caring for his aging parents and caring for his adult children who were returning home. He didn't face the issues of retirement. Or lingering illness. Or the deaths of many friends. He didn't see his children grow up and move far away. He didn't have to worry about the cost of catastrophic illness and whether low interest rates or inflation would eat away his life-savings. His own generation saw him as a "pioneer of faith," going where others had not been before. So he was. But many of you have had to be pioneers in faith, too, traveling ever more deeply into the ambiguity of the human situation. Those who would faithfully follow Jesus find that the trail he blazed comes to an abrupt end. Suddenly they find themselves where Jesus himself did not go and must then ask what it would mean to continue to follow him in spirit and in truth.

V

To say that Jesus lived an urgent life is certainly true. To say that he expected his own life to end prematurely is also true. But to say that Jesus lived with a short time horizon, as I have been doing so far today, may be more misleading than true. For while Jesus was intensely aware of the present and lived in the present, he certainly did not live for the present. He did not teach, as some gurus teach today, that this present moment— "the Now"—is all that we have. He knew that if we mistakenly think that the Now is all we have, our future may be eroded. Rather, Jesus understood that alongside this present moment— and ready to break in, uninvited and unannounced, at any moment—is a kind of time or a quality of time that for lack of a better word we sometimes call the Eternal. Jesus was thinking not only of the Now but also of the Eternal when he said this:

> Work urgently now, while it is still day. For the night is
> coming when no one will be able to work.

Jesus was saying this: Time as we know it often seems as though it will go on and on and on. But it won't. There is another dimension of life that is always near—that may break in now or may break in later—when it will break in we cannot predict—but when it does break in, it will change everything, utterly.

Jesus further understood that when this new dimension comes, it begins by slamming doors: "Work urgently now, while it is still day. For the night is coming when no one will be able to work."

When you were a child, did you play the game "Freeze"? Do you remember that? *Freeze!* When the new dimension comes—when what Jesus called the Eternal comes—it says, "Freeze." Suddenly, things that might have been changed a moment ago can no longer be changed. When the Eternal comes we discover that much of our freedom is gone, many doors are shut, and much in our life is suddenly fixed. I do not mean that no future doors will open, but they will not be the same doors. When the Eternal comes, certain things that might have been changed just a moment ago are suddenly and surprisingly frozen and fixed.

I saw Tonya Harding's ex-husband, Jeff Gillooly, on television the other night. In an interview he was seeing himself as going to jail now. He was seeing Tonya Harding's career as being over now. "How much money would you now give to roll the clock back to November?" the announcer asked, stupidly. Tears were rolling down Gillooly's face. "There's no amount of money I wouldn't give," he said. But money won't matter now. He knows that. Wishing won't matter now. For the Eternal has come, and much that was fluid is suddenly fixed.

VI

WE OURSELVES WILL know that the Eternal has come when the question "What do I want to do now?" absolutely pales before the question "What do I wish I had done?" Jesus did not live a hundred years, but he was not, therefore, a shallow, short-term thinker. With his whole body Jesus could feel that the Eternal was near. Therefore, he did "in the now" what he was happy to have done in "the end." In the lives of those who are wise, the questions "What do I want to do now?" and "What will I wish I had done in the end?" are not two questions but have somehow become one. May such a convergence increasingly occur in us.

February 1994

The Gift of Encouragement

◆　◆　◆

So Barnabas went to Tarsus to look for Saul; and
when he had found him, he brought him to Antioch.

— Acts 11:25–26a

L AST SATURDAY, I WAS completing a visit with my mother in
Milwaukee. She lives in a Christian retirement home
there and for the past several months has lived within
the health center of that home. My mother asked, if, before I
left, I would attend the Bible study that is held in the recreation
room on Saturday mornings. "I go whenever I feel able," she
said.

Hers is a large retirement home—two buildings and four
floors—that has grown since its modest beginnings in 1887.
When I was a child, I frequently went with my parents and
sister to that same home to visit my Great Aunt Laura, who was
bedridden there. The recreation room is in the south wing in
the basement, about as far from the Health Center as it could
possibly be, so for some of the residents getting there was quite
a trek. As we approached the room—my mother using her
walker and I pushing one of her friends in a wheelchair—I
could hear one of the residents playing an up-tempo version of
"Stand Up Stand Up for Jesus" and saw people coming from
several directions—some shuffling down hallways and others
popping out of elevators. There were about thirty participants
in all. Other than the chaplain and I, all were older women—
perhaps ten were in wheelchairs, ten used walkers, and ten
walked unassisted or with canes.

What occurred there was heartwarming to me. The residents sang a few hymns, and then the chaplain—a retired

Lutheran pastor—led them in an animated discussion of a few verses from the Book of Acts, in which most of the women participated. Along the way they had several chuckles and one or two belly laughs. One woman talked about her daughter who had broken several bones in a fall down a flight of stairs, the chaplain reminded them of an absent resident whose chemotherapy was not going well, and someone mentioned a new great-grandchild who was born during the previous week. Then they prayed, sang a hymn, received an ancient blessing and that was it. In an hour the Bible study was over and people began the shuffle or ride back to their rooms.

No one threw away her crutches that day. No one who arrived in a wheelchair left leaping and dancing. No one whose memory was shot full of holes on the way in had any more recall on the way out. No one who had been blind could now see. No one had turned off her hearing aid. Those who had been struggling with deciding what day it was before the Bible study were still uncertain. In that sense nothing had changed. But if you were sensitive to the mood of the group, you could detect that a lot had been transformed. On their way out, people were smiling and talking with one another, whereas they had been mostly silent on the way in. There was a lightness in the air—less of a feeling of being burdened. Some women pushed their walkers with a little more energy or zest. I thought I sensed within the participants a new spirit—perhaps, more accurately, a renewed spirit. They seemed more alive on the way out than they had been on the way in, and something inside me said, "Thank You, God" and "Hallelujah."

II

AFTER LITTLE EPISODES like that, my mind tends to take leaps—much like a flea jumping to a new dog. This time my mind remembered a middle-aged man who, when he found his life unraveling for yet another time, asked me, "When does the struggle stop? When does the difficulty end? How much longer must I grapple with life? How long will it be before I become a whole human being?" You'd like to be able to say, "Don't you see the light at the end of the tunnel?" but something else inside you knows better than that. Especially when you are watching people in a retirement home shuffle out of a Saturday morning Bible study. You get the definite impression that as long as we are living, there will be something with which to struggle—that as long as we are living, the universe will keep handing us a challenging agenda.

Then I started to think about that old question Christians used to enjoy asking each other—"Are you saved? Can you stand up at testimony meeting and say: 'Once I was crippled, but now I leap for joy; once I was blind, but now I see; once I was dead, but now I'm alive; once I was imprisoned, but now I am free'? Is that what has happened to you, brother or sister? Have you transcended the struggle? Are you now completely and unalterably new?" If those were the questions that had been asked of people as they left the Bible study group at the Milwaukee Protestant Home last Saturday, the answer in every instance would have been, "No." "How out of touch with reality are you?," someone might have asked as she tried to turn her walker around inside a cramped elevator, for it was obvious that no one had been delivered from her life situation. In that sense, no one had been "saved." Indeed, no one had gone there expecting to be saved. But what they had hoped for happened—they left the room encouraged. It is not theologi-cally correct to say this—but God helped me to see this, so I feel free to say it—human life being what it is, it is too much to ask to be saved from the human struggle. That struggle will con-tinue as long as we are alive. It is far wiser to feast on nourish-ment that is available day by day. It is far more faithful to allow ourselves simply to be encouraged. I saw that so plainly in Milwaukee last Saturday morning. The residents made their long trek to the Bible study, not to be saved, but to be encouraged. That's why my mother goes when she can—not to be delivered from her struggle, but to find energy for her struggle. She goes to be encouraged. And on that Saturday morning, I could tell that she, like many others, had been encouraged.

III

After I returned home, I began searching for the words "encourage," "encouraging" and "encouragement" in the Bible. I was surprised to find that they are rarely there. Instead, fancier and higher powered words like "salvation" and "redemption" keep showing up. You get the impression that something as temporary as encouragement was a phenomenon too puny to deserve much mention in the Holy Scriptures. The biblical writers seem more caught up in "all or nothing" type thinking—once I was dead, but now I'm alive; once I was despondent, but now I'm high on life; once I felt alienated, but now God and I are One." I must confess that I once thought in such grand categories. Religiously speaking, I was going for the bomb, swinging for the fences or hoping for a hole-in-one. Today I see what a gift and blessing it is simply to be encouraged. Others have done a lot for us, if they have helped us to be encouraged. We have done a lot for others, if we have helped them to be encouraged.

IV

One of the few places the word "encouragement" shows up in the Bible is within the New Testament story of Barnabas, which is recorded in the Book of Acts. You may not be familiar with Barnabas. He is prominent enough to be mentioned by name, but he is not seen as being one of the heavy hitters such as Peter, Paul, James or John. Yet, were it not for Barnabas, Christianity might not have so successfully expanded to the Gentile world, for it was Barnabas who paved the way for the one who would become the Apostle Paul.

Barnabas is interesting in that he is one of the several people in the Bible who have had their name changed to more adequately match their role or character: Abram became Abraham, Sarai became Sarah, Simon became Peter, Saul became Paul, and Joseph, a Jewish Levite from Cyprus, became known as Barnabas. Scholars disagree somewhat as to what "Barnabas" means, but the most frequent translation is "Son of Encouragement." A looser translation might be "One-Who-Has-the-Spirit-of-Encouragement" or "One Who Encourages." In the Book of Acts, Barnabas encourages in several ways. First, when the Jesus Movement was very young and was trying to get established in Jerusalem, Barnabas sold all of his property and gave that money to the apostles for them to use within the church. Second, when Saul, a persecutor of Christians, was converted to Christ on the Damascus Road, many were suspicious of him and thought him some sort of spy—a potential traitor. It was Barnabas, who went with Paul to Jerusalem, and helped to convince the leaders of the church that Paul had truly become a Christian disciple. He vouched for and stood alongside the still-suspect convert. Third, and perhaps most importantly, after Barnabas had gone to Antioch and had seen the potential for Christianity to take root and grow in the Greek world, he said to himself, "This is a task well suited for Paul," and he went to Tarsus, where Paul had been living in obscurity for twelve years, and brought him back to Antioch and used him to spearhead the Christian mission to the Gentiles. When there was a famine in Jerusalem, it was Barnabas with Paul, who collected an offering from distant churches and carried it to Jerusalem, so as to encourage the Christians there. Later, when a young disciple, John Mark, disappointed and angered Paul, Barnabas stood up for him and argued for John

Mark, just as he had earlier done for Paul. When Paul remained adamant that John Mark was not suitable for future service, Barnabas and Paul parted, with Barnabas taking John Mark as his assistant. When given this second chance, John Mark proved himself to be a faithful disciple.

Barnabas was a strong force in the early church, but he was not in the spotlight. The Bible calls him simply "a good man." He helped Christianity to spread through the ancient world by utilizing his ability to encourage others.

V

ENCOURAGE IS AN interesting word. Its opposite is "discourage." To discourage someone is to act toward them in such a way that it drains the courage out of them. To encourage a person is to act toward them in such a way that pours courage into them. Discouragement empties people; encouragement replenishes them.

I can imagine someone who is psychologically oriented saying that we can't expect other people to give us courage or blame others if we have lost our courage. Today it is "psychologically correct" to say that we must all be responsible for our own feelings, attitudes, moods, and emotions. If we lose our courage, our determination to go on and our willingness to continue the struggle, that's our own responsibility. It isn't someone else's fault.

That's certainly true in a way. If I allow others to empty me of my courage, that is my responsibility. Nevertheless, I am a human being, and I notice that whether I ought to be or not I am still affected by the way other people act toward me. Sometimes, because of what other people do, I am helped to continue, I am strengthened for the struggle, and I am given courage to face the challenges of human life.

For instance, last Friday morning the telephone rang at home before breakfast. It was a voice I'd not heard before. "Are you the person who does those short messages on the radio?" the caller asked. (I checked my watch and surmised that the caller must have just heard one.) I cautiously said, "Yes," not knowing what was going to come next. "I just want you to know that I appreciate those messages, and I'll bet a lot of other people do, too. They make me stop and think. I hope you keep doing them," she said. Did that phone call "save me" from the human situation? No. Did that phone call encourage me and give me a little more energy with which to deal with my situation? The answer, of course, is Yes.

VI

IN THE BIBLE, Barnabas encouraged the apostles by sharing money with them. He encouraged Paul by affirming him when others were suspicious and by remembering him, going to him, and inviting him to share in the Gentile mission. Barnabas encouraged the Christians in Jerusalem during a time of famine by collecting an offering and carrying it to them. And Barnabas encouraged John Mark by giving him a second chance after Paul had dismissed him.

Encouragement rarely results in headlines. It is a more humble kind of service. But seeing the renewed spirit among the women after the Bible study at the Milwaukee Protestant Home last Saturday, it occurred to me that in a world where we can almost never save one another, encouragement is one of the most precious gifts that we can give to one another. There are always many ways to encourage another. At home, at work, at school and within the church, I invite you to become, like Barnabas, a son or daughter of encouragement.

September 1994

Is the Sound of Truth
One Octave Too High?

◆ ◆ ◆

And the king of Israel said to Jehoshaphat, "Did I
not tell you that Micaiah would not prophesy
good concerning me, but evil?"

— I Kings 22:18

THE PROPHET AMOS is a good example of that handful of
intensely religious individuals within Israel who were
known as "prophets." The word "prophet" comes from
the Greek word *prophetes* and means literally "one who speaks on
behalf of," in this instance, "one who speaks on behalf of God."

Abraham J. Heschel, a prominent Jewish scholar, has written that the prophets were "some of the most disturbing
people who ever lived." They were disturbing because they told
the truth. They were disturbing because they told truths that
many people did not want to hear. They were disturbing
because they told their unpleasant truths forcefully and dramatically. Their message and manner of presentation com-
bined to cause most people to close their ears. As the chief
priest at Bethel said to King Jeroboam about Amos' prophecies:
"The land is not able to bear all his words." For this reason,
prophets were called "troublers of Israel."

II

ONE OF THE early prophets was named Micaiah. His story is told
in I Kings 22. In the episode that is related there, the King of

Israel and the King of Judah are getting ready to go to war against Syria to reclaim Ramoth-Gilead. They've decided that that piece of land belongs to them. Before they go to war the kings want to make sure that God is on their side, so they bring in one hundred prophets. These are not true prophets. They are "house prophets" who are on the payroll of the king. They do not speak on behalf of God, but make their living telling the king whatever he wants to hear. For the King of Israel to ask the house prophets whether God favored his going to war when he already had his helmet on was a lot like President Reagan asking Ollie North whether he thought it was a good idea to send arms to the Iran after he'd already signed the Ayatollah's Bible and baked him a cake. All one hundred house prophets agreed that the seizure of Ramoth-Gilead would be a good and easy thing. "Let's go, then!," the King of Judah said. But the King of Israel hesitated briefly for an interesting reason. He said, "There is one other prophet in these parts who is not on my payroll. Before we go we should probably hear from him. But I hate him because he never tells me anything good." So it was that Micaiah was brought before the king.

Much to the King of Israel's surprise, after he told Micaiah about the war that he planned to launch against Syria, Micaiah enthusiastically agreed with the hundred house prophets who had flattered the king. He said, "O wow, what an intelligent approach to international affairs, O King. Declaring war on a country so much bigger and stronger than our own. Fantastic! This will make our millennium. You have a genius for making wise decisions, King. If I were you, I'd go right now. I wouldn't even wait until morning. The sooner you leave, the sooner you can come back to celebrate the victory."

"Don't toy with me!," said the king. "I know you're lying. I know you don't think we'll win. Why are you lying to me?"

"O.K., I am lying!," said Micaiah. "I'm lying because going to war against Syria is such a stupid idea that it's hard for me to take it seriously. And I'm lying because the sooner you go, the sooner your army will be defeated and the sooner you'll be dead, so I won't have to put up with your foolishness ever again."

Now here's a little quiz. How do you think the biblical story ends?

> a) The King of Israel said to Micaiah, "Hmm, Micaiah, you state your position strongly, but I see the wisdom of it. Thanks for your forecast. We'll stay home and forget Ramoth-Gilead."

or

> b) The King of Israel was furious with Micaiah, had him thrown into prison for being insolent, and defiantly marched off to war, where his army was quickly scattered by the Syrians and where the king himself was killed.

How many say, a) "the king stayed home"? How many say, b) "the king marched off defiantly and was killed"? You're right! Option b accurately portrays the rest of the story. Micaiah was accurate in his predictions, but the king refused to hear. Where the prophets were concerned, people almost always refused to hear. It's as though the prophets' vocal cords vibrated at the frequency of dog whistles so that what they said went over or through everybody's heads. No, that's not quite right. A dog whistle is several octaves too high. The prophets spoke at a level that was one octave too high. The people heard the noise the prophets were making, but it hurt their ears. Thus, they did their best to shield themselves from the pain and to keep the prophet's message out of their heads.

III

IN THEOLOGICAL SEMINARY, professors tried to explain how shrill the prophets were—how offensive and off the wall they were considered in their own time—but I didn't quite comprehend it. However, a few years after I graduated I began to understand "shrill" when I found myself standing outside Milwaukee's City Hall with a Roman Catholic priest named Father Jim Groppi.

A number of people had gathered to express to the City Council their desire that the Council adopt a new ordinance that would begin to break up racially segregated housing patterns in that city. Milwaukee was the most segregated northern city in America at that time. When the TV cameras began to roll, Father Groppi picked up a microphone and began shouting up at the city hall in the direction of the Council Chambers. He was quoting from people like Amos, and John the Baptist, and Jesus but when directed toward the mayor and the aldermen, those words didn't sound as bland as they always did in church. Father Jim was shouting: "You brood of vipers, you bunch of poisonous snakes, you hypocrites! On the outside you're clean and bright like white-washed tombs, but inside you're filled with every kind of filth!"

I was sympathetic to the cause but I was shocked at how those biblical words were sounding in that setting. Jim looked and sounded like a raving lunatic—a Bible flopping in one hand and a microphone stabbing upward in the other—the cameras were rolling—this was going to make the six o'clock news—and I was standing right beside him. I was still in that stage of my ministry when I wanted to be loved and accepted by everyone and to my horror I was standing right beside him. Suddenly I had an existential understanding of what my seminary professors meant when they said that Israel's prophets were shrill.

What kind of individuals are those who shriek and shout in public—who call people ugly names just because they prefer segregated housing patterns, or just because they rip people off, or just because they are cheating in business or are taking bribes in government, or just because they are destroying the environment, or just because they are peddling drugs, or just because they are wanting to sell automatic weapons to teenagers on the street, or just because they are turning their backs on the poor? What kind of folks get steamed up about things like that?

Or is the question, "What kind of people don't get steamed up about things like that?" How shall we describe people who don't give a hoot about things like that?

IV

I LEARNED SOMETHING new about shrill this week. I learned that messages can be shrill even when there is nothing high-pitched about their presentation. I saw that for myself on Friday afternoon, when I returned to the office and checked my voice mail. One message was fine. I noted it and shortly thereafter returned the call. But when the second message came on, it was instant pain. It was as though someone were blowing a police whistle into the phone, one octave too high. I pulled back from it immediately, trying to close off my hearing before the message got through. When I couldn't deafen myself in time, I fast-forwarded the message. I haven't listened to the message in its entirety yet.

The message wasn't shouted, it wasn't shrieked. It was a human voice, calm and well-modulated. But the message itself shrieked. The message itself screamed at me. For the caller was asking when I'm going to have a project finished that is already overdue. Other people are waiting for me and depending on me, he said. That wasn't a message I wanted to hear right then. It's been a busy week and weekend. I'm leaving town at 6:00 o'clock on Tuesday morning and will be gone much of the month. I hadn't even been thinking about this project. There are several other things higher on my priority list that I must also do before Tuesday morning. If you listened to the message on my voice mail, you would think it a normal message. But for me, it was a message that shouted—a message one octave too high—a message that shrieked. This message was painful because it is true. The caller was right: the project is overdue, other people are depending on me, and I promised that I would complete it. I don't know how I'll complete it by Tuesday morning at 6:00, but the message is true, nevertheless.

Let's have another quiz. I'll ask you to vote in just a moment. What do you think? Again, you have two options.

a) In the long run, will my life be better if I do everything I can to stay busy with other things, and get out of town Tuesday morning without returning the message, hoping that the caller won't reach me until August?

b) In the long run will my life be better if I march myself into the office early this afternoon, face the music, and figure out how, in the time I have available, I can faithfully respond to this message?

Pretend you are true prophets. How many say, a) "Sneak out of town"? How many say, b) "Face the music"? There's a big majority in favor of facing the music. See! That's why true prophets were considered so obnoxious.

V

My point is a simple one. I notice that, like the King of Israel in the Micaiah story or Amaziah in the Amos story, there are lots of truths in life that I don't want to hear. I do my best to shut those truths out—I flinch—just as I would if someone were blowing a police whistle, one octave too high, right in my ear. I have a hunch that at times you flinch like that, too.

Painful truth—that is, truth that is demanding a change in us—is always one octave too high. It hurts us to listen. The prophets were shrill—they did all they could to get people's attention—because people were ignoring more subtle messages and because they understood that painful truths will eventually hurt us, much, much more if we do not muster the courage to listen to them at the earliest possible time. True prophets were shrill and disturbing because they believed it is always best to face the music—it is always best to go eyeball to eyeball with the truth—at the earliest possible time.

July 1995

Disturbing the Peace

◆　◆　◆

These men are Jews and they are disturbing
our city.

— Acts 16:20

T HE DAY BEGAN peacefully enough, but by nightfall Paul,
Silas and the other Jews, who were proclaiming Jesus as
the Christ, had their feet fastened in stocks within a
prison, after having been attacked by a crowd, charged by
magistrates, and beaten by police. They had been seeking
converts in Macedonia during one of Paul's missionary jour-
neys. As the day began, he and the others were returning to the
place of prayer beside a river on the outskirts of Philippi where
they had met and baptized Lydia the previous week. In those
times, Jews often placed their synagogues or prayer places near
moving water. In a similar fashion, early Christians preferred to
baptize in moving water—the more swiftly the water moved,
the greater the spiritual efficacy. Centuries later this ancient
Jewish practice of worshipping near moving water was frequently adopted for use by rural Christians in our country.
Hence, we have early American hymns such as, "We shall
gather at the river, the beautiful, beautiful river" and "Down by
the riverside." Such human gravitations toward water have
been experienced in all generations. As Wallace Stegner asked
after reading Norman Maclean's story, "A River Runs Through
It," "Who is not haunted by waters?" I certainly am.

II

WHILE PAUL AND the others were walking toward the river on the sabbath day, a slave girl with an unusual spirit began to follow them. From the way her behavior is described it seems fair to say that, in part, the slave girl was afflicted with a "disturbed spirit" or a "troubled spirit." Some translations say "an evil spirit." William Barclay, the Scottish Bible scholar, is more colloquial and says flat out that she was "mad."

One afternoon last week, I was waiting for the light to change at a crosswalk downtown, when I heard a disturbance coming from the corner diagonally opposite. There a middle-aged woman was angrily shouting at a car. No one in the car spoke back to the woman. Those two people seemed confused as to why she was shouting at them. Then the woman abruptly turned away from that car and briskly crossed Fourth Street against the light. She continued shouting, but now she was shouting at herself or perhaps at some voices she was hearing within herself. There's no question in my mind that if I'd been on her side of the street, she'd also have been shouting at me. By her behavior and appearance I concluded, rightly or wrongly, that whatever was triggering the disturbance was inside the woman herself. She struck me as being chronically ill, mentally. I thought it possible that she'd stopped taking her anti-hallucinatory medicine.

That kind of muttering, shouting dialogue with invisible events or inner voices is one kind of symptom that biblical people associated with being possessed by a demon. Today we would be more likely to say that such a person was emotionally disturbed or was manifesting a troubled spirit. To understand the slave girl in this biblical story you might begin by imagining someone shouting angrily at herself or at oncoming cars while crossing a busy street against the light in heavy traffic.

III

HOWEVER, WHILE THE Bible shows the slave girl as having a troubled spirit, it says that the spirit within her was a spirit of divination. To divine things means to discover truths without resorting to what most people would consider necessary tangible evidence. To divine things is to sense things or to predict things through the use of omens, intuition or the ability to pick up on unseen vibrations.

One summer when I was a boy, my family vacationed in the north woods near the cottage of one of my parents' friends. He was needing to dig a new well. As a way of locating the best spot to dig it, he cut a fresh, green branch from a willow tree in the shape of a wish bone, held and twisted both ends in his hands and then walked back and forth over his property waiting for the end of the branch to twitch. He was trying to pick up invisible, underground vibrations that would tell him where the water was. After walking back and forth for about a half-an-hour, crisscrossing his property, he drove a stake and said, "This is where we'll dig." His branch, of course, was a divining rod. The slave girl in our story didn't have a divining rod, she was a divining rod. Somehow her body read clues very easily. She could even sense the future with unusual accuracy. If we think of divination as being closely linked with the divine, we won't be far from the ancient mind. Again, William Barclay reports that the ancient world showed a strange respect for people who were mad, for, as they said, "the gods had taken away their wits to put the minds of the gods into them." In the ancient world it was believed that mentally ill people could see and sense things that others couldn't see.

I don't know if you have had opportunity to interact with mentally ill persons close up, but sometimes people who are in a psychotic state have amazing clarity about certain things. I recall a time many years ago when I was locked within a small room inside a psychiatric ward with a man who was having a full-blown manic episode. While he was wildly out of touch with some realities, he was very much in touch with other realities. He was particularly lucid about me and demonstrated a keen ability to see into me. Without pulling any punches, he turned me inside out and scathingly told me lots about my inner self that I would have preferred no one be able to see. This man was blind to his own limitations, but in his manic state, he could certainly see my limitations. Likewise, the slave girl described in the Book of Acts who had a disturbed spirit also had an uncanny ability to sense and see.

From the description the Bible gives, we can further assume that this young girl had a war going on inside her—a struggle between the divine and the demonic. Nevertheless, her owners did not want her soothed or healed. They sold her predictions to people who were drawn to gambling or speculation. She was a crystal ball on wheels. She was a walking, talking, shouting fortune cookie. She was a tantalizing tip on every race. Further, she was low maintenance. Her owners provided her with room and board and kept all the profits. That's the picture the biblical writer expects us to have when he mentions a slave girl with a spirit of divination.

IV

WHEN THE SLAVE girl saw Paul and the others, she didn't forecast the future, but immediately tuned into something that others in the crowd were missing and began expressing it. She followed Paul and his co-workers for several days, crying out, "These men are servants of the Most High God, who proclaim to you the way of salvation. These men are servants of the Most High God, who proclaim to you the way of salvation." She had, of course, divined the truth but Paul grew tired of hearing her shouting it. The Bible says that Paul became annoyed after this had been going on for several days. (That gives some insight into what the church means by a saint. When the we say that the Apostle Paul was a saint we don't mean to imply that he was the kind of person who was never annoyed, but the kind of person who didn't get annoyed the first few days.) Eventually, Paul was annoyed and turning to the woman, said to the spirit, "I charge you in the name of Jesus Christ to come out of her!" Then we're told that the spirit came out of her that very hour. Not living in the ancient world, we might say "she regained her sanity" in that very hour.

What are we to make of this aspect of the story? It causes me to recall a time years ago when I was asked to assist a woman who was experiencing a severe psychotic episode during a time of unusual stress. A year earlier she had suffered similar symptoms and had been hospitalized for three months. Once again she was profoundly agitated. I'm not sure what possessed me, but when her friend left the room to call an ambulance I looked her in the eye, called her by name, and asked, "What are you doing?" Instantly, she stopped shouting, looked me in the eye and calmly said, "I'm acting crazy." Not being as bold as Paul, I didn't command the disturbed spirit to come out of her, but I did call her by name and said, "ok, be as crazy as you must, but get back in your right mind as soon as you can."

I'd like to report that the ambulance was then no longer needed, but after a brief pause in which I could see her brain's inner wheels turning, she started acting crazy again. This time, however, she wasn't gone for three months, but returned to her right mind and to her home in three days. She has stayed in her right mind ever since, living a full, satisfying and creative life. I don't know if our exchange had anything whatsoever to do with her accelerated healing, but the memory of her coming to her normal senses, however briefly, to quietly say, "I'm acting crazy," makes it easy for me to believe the Bible when it says of the slave girl that in response to Paul's command she regained her sanity in that very hour.

V

NOW, HERE'S THE RUB. When the girl lost her demon she also lost some of her special gifts. The war within her was ended, but her body was no longer a divining rod. She could offer no tips regarding corn futures or the big fifty mile chariot race held each year in Ephesus. Her owners, who saw their profits flying right out the window, were so angry that they hauled Paul and Silas before the magistrates. They accused them of breaking Roman laws and disturbing the peace. People in the crowd who had been purchasing her predictions were likewise enraged. They fell upon Paul and Silas, ripping their clothes off them and beating them. Even the authorities became furious, inflicting many blows with rods and throwing them into jail. That was lots of uproar and serious punishment for casting out one disturbed spirit. The Bible doesn't say whether or not the slave girl herself joined in beating them.

Do you find it interesting that in Bible stories there is so much resistance to people being healed. That was true during Jesus' ministry as well as during the ministries of Paul and Silas. To refresh your memory of just one such example, when Jesus healed the disturbed man known as the Gerasene demoniac, the crowd didn't inflict blows on Jesus, but they did demand that he get back in his boat and immediately leave the region. The authorities in the Temple were offended when Jesus opened the eyes of the man who had been born blind. Often after Jesus healed a person, onlookers were upset. It was always the wrong person, or the wrong method, or the wrong place, or the wrong time. Even some people who were themselves in need of liberation from demons became alarmed when Jesus came into the room, and told him to go away from them. In this story, the people objected when Paul freed the slave girl, just as people often complained when Jesus disturbed the peace. Is this why, when Jesus healed ten lepers, only one came back to say,

"Thank you"? Did the other nine not come back because they weren't grateful? Was there something they liked about being sick? Was there something they enjoyed about being exiled? When he healed those nine lepers, did they see Jesus as having disturbed their peace?

VI

ALL THIS SUGGESTS to me, that as human beings, we can get used to almost anything. We can enter into some very strange agreements with ourselves, or with others, or life so as to maintain what appears to us to be "the peace." For example, in *New World, New Mind,* ecologist Paul Erhlich tells about flying into Los Angeles and meeting a friend at the airport on a summer night. Erlich couldn't believe how smoggy it was, with huge halos around all the parking lot lights. Sarcastically, he said, "What a beautifully clear night." His friend who lived in LA missed the sarcasm and said, "Yes, it hasn't been clear like this for several weeks." Erhlich concluded that over time we can get used to almost anything. We may even (as the Bible reminds us) resent anyone who would change things—who would disturb what we believe to be our peace.

As a result of pondering this story, the insight I'm trying to come to grips with is the biblical fact that Paul and Silas—that Jesus Christ—that God—favor disturbing our peace, if it is an uneasy peace. Sometimes it feels as though we will die, if our peace is disturbed. But it may be that we have accommodated ourselves to a false peace, an uneasy peace. That kind of peace may need to be disturbed so that we can be more fully, more freely, and more authentically alive.

May 1995

When Wounds Are Transformed

◆　◆　◆

Put your finger here, and look at my hands;
reach out your hand and put it in my side.

— John 20:27

T HE FIRST TIME the Risen Christ appeared to his disciples in
an upper room in Jerusalem, the door was locked because of fear. The disciples were hiding from the authorities. I imagine them huddled together, listening for a
creaking stair or for the clanging of armor and the shuffle of
feet on the city street below. When someone did come it was
not the authorities but Jesus Christ in his risen power. Those
who were present fully believed in his appearance and when
Thomas, who had been absent, returned, they said to him
excitedly, "We have seen the Lord!"

It is interesting to me that when the Risen Christ returned
the second time a week later, all the disciples were still inside
the upper room and the door was still closed. They may not
have been quite as afraid as before, but they were not sufficiently confident or courageous to unlock the door—not to
mention daring to peer out into the hallway. Only Thomas,
who had difficulty believing, apparently had the courage to
come and go—else how could he have been absent at the time
of Christ's first appearance?

That the disciples remained behind locked doors suggests
that in their own lives Easter was a long time dawning. Eventually they would courageously and openly stand up to the
authorities that they had feared initially. For example, in the
Book of Acts, it says, "When the crowds saw the boldness of
Peter and John they knew that they had been with Jesus." But

that boldness had not yet arisen in them. It took the disciples a period of time to assimilate their experience of Jesus as the Risen Christ. While they labored to take in this belief, they apparently weren't able to live it out. Be that as it may. Jesus found them a second time. He had an easier time entering the locked upper room than they had leaving it.

Thomas, you'll remember, had complained that he wouldn't believe that Jesus had risen until he examined physical evidence. "Unless I see the scars of the nails in his hands and put my finger on those scars and my hand in his side, I will not believe," he had said. So when Jesus did appear before Thomas he said to him, "Put your finger here, and look at my hands; reach out your hand and put it in my side. Stop your doubting and believe!"

Notice that even though Jesus had been resurrected, his wounds remained visible. Not only were Jesus' wounds real initially, but death and resurrection did not erase the effect that life in this world had on him.

When I was a boy I was given a toy called a magic slate. It was a tablet with a gray film that was covered with a celuloid sheet. I wrote on the slate with a wooden stick. To erase what I had written, it was only necessary to pull up the gray sheet. That had a characteristic sound. Something like, Rrrrrrrp! I recall those magic slates sometimes when I've had a conversation with someone in which I thought we agreed on an outcome, but nothing happened afterwards. Sometimes you can have a meeting of the minds, but that's all you have. As you go out the door, the other person is magic slating you. I can sometimes hear the slate being erased as I go out the door—Rrrrrrrp!

That Jesus showed up after his death still bearing his scars and wounds strongly suggests—poetically, if not scientifically— that whatever we're writing our lives on, it isn't a magic slate. Our experiences in this life, this story implies, help to shape who we will be in any future life.

Further, although Jesus still had his wounds he was able to invite Thomas to put his fingers and hands in them. This tells me that while the old wounds were still present, they were not burning or throbbing. The former agonizing pain had vanished. This is part of what it means to be in a resurrected state. Perhaps we could go so far as to say that when we arrive at a point where we still have our wounds but no longer suffer the old agonizing pain, we, too, will have been raised with Christ to a new plane of life altogether. This is in contrast to carrying both our old wounds and our old pain.

I recall being in a group several years ago in which a number of single people were gathering for the first time and were introducing themselves. "Tell a little about yourself," the leader said. Most people did just that, but one man told a great deal about himself. In particular he talked with great anger and hurt about the way his wife had left him. His pain and rage filled the room in which we were sitting. "When did that happen to you?, the leader then asked. "Eight years ago!," the man said. This man had been wounded—there was no doubt about it. But not only was he carrying his old wounds with him, he was still carrying the pain in a very active sense. The pain of eight years before was still being experienced in the present tense. Without judging this man, let me simply say that eight years after his wife left him he was still being crucified. He had not yet experienced the resurrected state.

Jesus was in the resurrected state. You and I can know that we also are in the resurrected state when our old wounds don't hurt us in that terrible way any more.

Finally, when Thomas saw Jesus' wounds and touched the wounds, his own despair and unbelief were healed. Thomas fell down on his knees and believed. This strongly suggests that when we are in the resurrected state—that is, when we still bear evidences of having been wounded but are no longer in the old agonizing pain—the hurts we have experienced can be a healing resource for others.

Carlo Carretto, a desert monk who suffered many deprivations, once said:

> When the flood of pain has passed over a soul,
> what remains alive can be considered genuine.

John's Gospel tells us that by the time Jesus had returned to the upper room the flood of pain had already passed over his soul. Jesus did not seek to avoid that flood, but experienced it and weathered it. He rode it out to the end. Then somehow—I can't begin to say how—the agonizing pain passed. Somehow Jesus moved beyond that pain. He could say, "Here, Thomas, put your fingers in my hands; place your hand in my side."

Last year I read a book of stories by Tim O'Brien called *The Things They Carried*. These are all Vietnam stories. Tim O'Brien fought in Vietnam, and for twenty years he has mostly written Vietnam stories. This was the most moving and powerful book that I read last year. It is very haunting and still affects me. Somehow this book is different than other Vietnam books— even Tim O'Brien's earlier works. In talking about the book with a friend this week, I finally realized why this book is different. The wounds are still there—"Here, Thomas, see and touch my hands and side"—but somehow the most agonizing pain is gone. The bitterness, the rage, the hatred and the self-pity seem to be gone. Somehow the flood of pain that entered his soul twenty years ago seems to have passed over his soul— leaving him not untouched and not weaker, but stronger for having been wounded. What is still alive is genuine. And what is still alive and genuine has a mysterious ability to uplift and heal.

Don't think about this kind of resurrection as a demand or an obligation, but as a God-given possibility. We have all been wounded. You have had your hurts and I have had mine. Our hurts vary and are not of the same degree. It may even be that after a long time our hurts still feel fresh and are still very much with us. What is possible is that one day they won't be. God heals. God raises up. The flood passes over our soul. One day what had been a fresh wound becomes largely scar and memory. Yes, we were wounded, but somehow we have been relieved of our most burning pain. To our surprise, we will then discover that we have within ourselves a new capacity to help others—a new power to heal.

April 1991

Restoration

◆　◆　◆

"Behold, Lord, the half of my goods I give
to the poor."
— Luke 19:8

MY FATHER HAD a generous spirit and a big heart, but one leg was shorter than the other, he walked with a painful limp, was not tall, and thought of himself as a small man. I've always assumed that that's why the story of Zacchaeus, a man whom the Bible says was small of stature, was one of his favorite stories. My father also worked with money, and although I can't imagine that my father ever cheated anyone, he may have felt that handling money was something else that he and Zacchaeus had in common. It's also easy for me to imagine my father shinnying up a sycamore tree, if that's what it took to see Jesus.

However, if Jesus had come to my father's town, you wouldn't have found my father up in a sycamore tree. Because of the way my father felt about Jesus, you would have found him in the front row, sitting on the curb or in a collapsible lawn chair. My father would have been one of the first to arrive. So, the fact that Zacchaeus didn't get to the parade route until the streets were lined with onlookers several rows deep tells us something. It suggests that this was a last minute decision on his part. Luke plainly says that it was not love of Jesus, but curiosity about Jesus that drew him there. When Zacchaeus realized that he wouldn't see Jesus from behind the fourth row, even by stretching and bouncing up on his toes, he climbed into a tree farther up the road above where Jesus soon would be passing.

II

I'VE HEARD PREACHERS say because Zacchaeus was a chief tax collector and very rich, that sitting in a tree above a parade route with his feet dangling was out of character for him and that townspeople were no doubt surprised to see him there. That's probably right. It's hard to imagine a major bureaucrat swallowing a sufficient amount of pride to perch up there. Indeed, such behavior was so out of character for Zacchaeus that I suspect that he was surprised to find himself up there. When he saw the people whose taxes he collected looking up at him with strange expressions on their faces, it's easy to imagine him asking himself, "What am I doing here?"

Have there been times in your life when you didn't quite know why you were where you were? Have you ever scratched your head and asked, "What am I doing here?" That has happened to me in a variety of settings, but seems to happen most frequently in my own kitchen between the hours of nine or ten o'clock in the evening when I find myself standing in front of an open refrigerator door for no apparent reason. I don't know why I'm there. I just notice that I am there, peering into the refrigerator searchingly, as though there was some purpose for my visit.

This week I heard a woman my age speak of her own such visits to the refrigerator and she attributed them to the aging process. That is clearly an erroneous interpretation. I know that it isn't brain cells flaking off that causes this, because the first time I caught myself staring mindlessly into a refrigerator I was not yet twenty-one years old. If you stare into open refrigerators occasionally now, that's not necessarily a matter of aging. You probably did that before you were thirty, although you may not realize it because people who stare into open refrigerators are not known for their heightened consciousness. My theory is that when Zacchaeus found himself sitting in a sycamore tree and asked "What am I doing here?" he felt as you and I do when we find that we have walked to the refrigerator for no apparent reason. Yes, he'd gone to see who Jesus was, but what was going on inside of Zacchaeus that caused him to be curious? I'm not sure that Zacchaeus fully understood what was pulling him toward Jesus and pushing him up into a sycamore tree.

III

Israel's great prophet, Elijah, would tell us that the question "What am I doing here?" can be an important spiritual question coming from a place that is deeper than consciousness. You may recall that "What are you doing here?" is the question that Elijah was able to hear only after the fleeing prophet had spent many days hiding in the wilderness. When you and I are standing at a refrigerator door for no apparent reason, something more than forgetfulness may be occurring. Something deep within us—our heart, our soul, our unconscious, or our deepest self—may be signaling a need, a hunger, a thirst, an uneasiness, or an emptiness of which our conscious self is not yet even dimly aware. It isn't only open refrigerator doors or sycamore trees that do this. Sometimes people go the Mall, or watch television, or eat another bowl of ice cream, or buy a more expensive car, or order another round of drinks, or have an extra-marital affair because there is a spiritual restiveness within them of which they are not yet consciously aware. I believe that Zacchaeus was drawn to Jesus for a reason. It's just that Zacchaeus didn't know the reason. However, when Jesus came by and looked up at him, Jesus could see the reason and said, "Come down, Zacchaeus; I'm going to spend some time at your house today." Out of all the people gathered there that day, why did Jesus pick Zacchaeus? Because, as Jesus emphasized at the end of this story, he came to save those who were lost—that is, he came to be helpful to those who didn't know why they were where they were in life—be they standing in front of an open refrigerator, cruising the Mall or sitting in a sycamore tree.

IV

THE BIBLE DOES not tell us what Jesus and Zacchaeus talked about when they were inside the tax collector's house or how their relationship unfolded, but I am fascinated with what each of them said when they came out of the house. I see the situation to be quite similar to the press conferences the President holds in the Rose Garden after an important meeting with a state visitor. First, Zacchaeus reports to the crowd how things will be different because of the visit and then Jesus comments.

After Zacchaeus tells Jesus in public how he plans to change, you don't need to be a psychotherapist to understand what had been bothering him below the level of consciousness. For when their visit was over, Zacchaeus stood and said: "Behold, Lord, the half of my goods I give to the poor; and if I have defrauded anyone of anything, I restore it fourfold."

It was his wealth that was bothering Zacchaeus—the discrepancy between what he had and what many others didn't have. Not just the fact of his wealth, but the way he knew he had gathered it. Where he could return to an individual what he had fraudulently taken, he would do so directly, fourfold. And for the many instances in which the particular wrong could no longer be righted, he would make a general restoration, giving half of his goods to the poor.

Notice then what Jesus says. Jesus doesn't say, "Because you are going back to undo your wrongs as best you can, I will love you, save you and forgive you." No, Jesus has already loved Zacchaeus. Instead, Jesus said, "Because of what you have chosen to do, I see that salvation has come to this house today." Do you see? The fact that Zacchaeus will undo as many of his wrongs as he can is evidence to Jesus that Zacchaeus is saved—saved from caring less about honesty than riches, saved from his fraud and his greed, saved from having to use half of his energy trying to forget the manner in which he gained his riches. The fact that Zacchaeus will undo as many of his wrongs as he can is evidence to Jesus that Zacchaeus is being healed, that Zacchaeus is becoming whole, that Zacchaeus is finally getting his life together. Jesus doesn't love Zacchaeus because he is getting his life together, but Zacchaeus is getting his life together because, after being with Jesus, he understands that he, too, is a son of Abraham—that he, too is one of God's children—that he, too, is unconditionally valued and loved.

V

ZACCHAEUS' RESPONSE TO God's love and forgiveness, which came to him through Jesus, is very Jewish. That's one of the basic ways that Judaism teaches its people to respond to any sin. First, you reflect on it and try to understand why you did it. You also try to feel the pain of the injury you have done, all in an attempt to lessen the chance that you will do it again. But then you go back to whomever was injured and make restoration as best you can. Sometimes you can't fix the hurt you have done—it's too late or the damage was irreversible—but you find some way to signal your sorrow, your desire to heal and your decision to move forward in a new way.

Here's a small example in my own life. One I'm willing to talk about here. Recently, I have had occasion to remember a boy who lived in my neighborhood and was a classmate of mine in high school. I played football and track and hung out with the "in crowd," but my acquaintance Nathaniel didn't. I didn't consciously try to injure Nat, but I did nothing to make life easier for him. Even though we were neighbors, I pretty much ignored him. He studied a lot; he didn't play sports; I thought him something of a wimp. After high school, I didn't hear about Nat until late in the Vietnam War when a story about him went out over the news services. It seems that Nat was an Army surgeon in Vietnam. One day medics brought in a soldier who had a live grenade buried in his intestines. Nat volunteered to try to remove it. They protected his body with heavy flak jackets but there was no way to remove the grenade without using his surgeon's hands. If the grenade had exploded

Nat would have lost his forearms and his hands, but he saved the infantryman's life by removing the grenade safely. As you would expect, that news changed my whole picture of Nat. I wasn't even in the war. If anyone was a wimp, I was the wimp. I had judged him unfairly. I decided to write him a letter to express the respect and admiration that I belatedly felt for him. But I got busy with something else and never wrote him. Six months later, when home on leave in Milwaukee visiting his young children, Nat was killed by a hit-and-run driver while crossing a street. Lately I have been thinking of him.

Now, certainly Nat wasn't sitting in Nam waiting for my letter—I don't know how much pain, if any, I created for him in high school by depreciating him and holding him at arms length—and I fully understand that there is now nothing that I can do for him. But it occurs to me that in Milwaukee some of his relatives may still be living—surely his children are still living—and I could tell them how moved I was by his heroism—and perhaps they would tell me where he is buried and I could spend a few moments silently standing beside his grave. I might even talk to him. Not so God will love me. God already loves me. But to help me not do that again. To help me to move forward more faithfully, more compassionately and less judgmentally. To make my own life a little less broken and a little more complete.

VI

RECENTLY, MY DAUGHTER, Sarah, and I watched a home video of *Heart and Soul,* a film about two men and two women who were killed in a bus accident and, before moving on to heaven, were given extra time in which to go back and resolve their lives "by doing the one thing that would make their lives complete." The four characters used their time in various ways: A thief returned $100,000 worth of stamps that he had stolen from a young boy; a timid and cowardly singer sang The Star-Spangled Banner to cheering crowds at a rock concert; a mother helped reconnect her son with his long-lost sisters; and a woman who had lost a love relationship by undervaluing it, when finding that her lover was dead, helped a young man not lose his girlfriend through carelessness. The movie was entertaining, but raised for me the question of my own unfinished deeds. What one thing would I hurry back to do, if I were given extra time? Zacchaeus arrived at his answer in one afternoon, but I'm giving myself time to sit with that question.

What about you? If you suddenly died and were given an extra chance, what would you hurry back to do? Is there a wrong that you would try to right? A debt that you would repay? A love that you would express? A wasted opportunity that you would finally grasp? An injury that you would try to heal? And if you would hurry back to do it then, why not now? If there is something that would make your life more complete, is there any way to do it now? Not so God will love you—God loves you already—but so that you may be more whole and your life more complete.

July 1995

Treasure Worth Having

◆　◆　◆

Do not lay up for yourselves treasures on earth,
where moth and rust consume and
where thieves break in and steal . . .

— Matthew 7:19

WHAT IN LIFE is worth having? Actually, that's not quite the way I want to ask the question. There is so much in life that has some value. Let me ask that again: What in life is most worth having?

Do you remember the crusty old cow poke in the film *City Slickers* who raised his index finger to tell Billy Crystal that life (when best understood) is about one thing? You may recall that he died before saying what that one thing was. If your life had to be about only one thing, which one thing would you pick?

The price we pay for whatever it is that we are pursuing in life is, of course, our life. All we really have to spend is our life. We speak of spending our time and that is exactly what we are doing with it. Every twenty-four hours we spend twenty-four hours of our life. When we spend our time, or our energy, or our money, we are, in fact, spending our life. What in life is worth the expenditure of your life?

There is much available in life that is not worth the expenditure of your life. Have you ever spent a portion of your life on something that seemed a bargain at the time, but later proved not to be worthy of your life? What would it mean to spend yourself only in ways that are worthy of your life?

All the questions that I have been asking are the kind of questions that Jesus asked people again and again. It was a major theme in his teaching. Lots of Jesus' talk about the

Kingdom of God or the Kingdom of heaven—especially when using the metaphors of a pearl of great price or a treasure hidden in a field—was really a way of asking "Which of the many treasures available in life is actually worth your life?" Heavenly treasure is treasure that does not fade, even in the light of eternity. Heavenly treasure is anything that we are able to treasure, even though it costs our life.

II

HAVE I TOLD YOU about the pirate ring I bought at a market in Juárez, Mexico, when I was a boy of ten? On vacation I'd gone with my parents and sister to El Paso to visit my Uncle Billy in Texas. While there, we crossed the border and went shopping in Juárez. We weren't in the market long before my eyes focused on a copper-colored ring that I thought pretty nifty. It had a skull and crossbones on it. My father said I'd probably be sorry if I bought it. I thought he was objecting to the skull and crossbones, but what he said was that it looked like it would turn my finger green. I thought that fear preposterous. How could a ring turn your finger green? Later in the day, while my father stood nearby silently, I bought it. Since my father didn't understand just how nifty my new pirate ring was, I proudly showed it to my Uncle Billy. He looked at it and said, "It looks like it will turn your finger green."

In the face of my elders' lack of enthusiasm, I simmered all the way back to El Paso and became even more annoyed when, before I went to bed, I saw that the ring was turning black and my finger was turning green. For a few days I polished the ring frequently and washed my hands a lot to hide the black and the green. When I saw that it was a losing battle, I stopped wearing the ring and tucked it in my suitcase. To my father's credit, he never asked me why my finger looked so green.

Whether as a child or an adult, have you ever spent a portion of your life on something that seemed a bargain at the time, but later proved not to be such a wise investment? Jesus said:

> Do not lay up for yourselves treasures on earth, where moth and rust consume and where thieves break in and steal, but lay up for yourselves treasures in heaven, where neither moth nor rust consumes and where thieves do not break in and steal.

Jesus is making two points here. First, spend yourself on treasures that will endure—not on things that will rot or rust away. Second, invest in things that no one can take away from you. That second point is especially provocative: invest in things that no one can take away from you. What do you suppose Jesus meant by that? What kinds of things could you invest in that no one could take away from you?

III

WHEN JESUS URGES his followers to stop worrying about earthly things—that is, to stop obsessing about their own security issues and to instead be concerned about heavenly treasure—he leaves most people in our culture behind. Often it seems that we care about earthly security and earthly treasure most of all. Contemporary philosopher Jacob Needleman has said this in *Money and the Meaning of Life.*

> In other times and places, not everyone has wanted money above all else; people have desired salvation, beauty, power, strength, pleasure, propriety, explanations, food, adventure, conquest, comfort. But here and now, money—not necessarily even the things money can buy, but money is what everyone wants.

In their bestseller, *Your Money or Your Life,* Joe Dominquez and Vicki Robin say this:

> Money is something we choose to trade our life energy for.... Our allotment of time here on earth, the hours of precious life available to us.

Another observer, David Korten, adds:

> We consistently undervalue the life energy we put into ob-
> taining money. [We act as though] Our purpose is to con-
> sume—that we were born to shop.

This is not a new accusation. Perhaps it has always seemed so to
the spiritually minded. Two thousand years ago, Jesus said that
"all the nations of the world" are passionately concerned about
security issues—about what to eat, and what to drink, and
where to sleep, and what to put on. Don't be like them, Jesus
said to his followers. Instead, seek riches that endure. Instead,
pursue treasures that no one can take away from you. What are
the riches that endure, do you think? What are the treasures
that no one can take away from you? Do you already have
some treasures that no one can take away from you? I suspect
that you have. It is important that you recognize and name
them. What treasures do you already have that no one can take
away from you?

The sixth chapter of Second Corinthians includes my
favorite passage written by the Apostle Paul. I find it to be a
lovely passage. Let me read part of it to you from the J. B.
Phillips translation. This passage makes it so clear that it is
possible for human beings to live rewarding lives without being concerned most of all about money or about their own
security.

> We want to prove ourselves genuine ministers of God what-
> ever we have to go through—patient endurance of troubles
> or even disasters, being flogged or imprisoned; being mobbed,
> having to work like slaves, having to go without food or
> sleep. All this we want to meet with sincerity, with insight
> and patience; by sheer kindness and the Holy Spirit; with
> genuine love, speaking the plain truth, and living by the
> power of God. Our sole defense, our only weapon, is a life of
> integrity, whether we meet honor or dishonor, praise or
> blame. Called "impostors" we must be true, called "nobod-
> ies" we must be in the public eye. Never far from death, yet
> here we are alive, always "going through it" yet never "going

under." We know sorrow, yet our joy is inextinguishable. We have "nothing to bless ourselves with" yet we bless many others with true riches. [And then my favorite line.] We are penniless, and yet in reality we have everything worth having.

What do you imagine that a person has when he or she can say, "We are penniless, and yet in reality we have everything worth having"? If you were in danger and were penniless, what would you be willing to call "everything worth having"?

I have been asking you questions persistently today, because you are the only one who can decide which treasures are worth your life. Only you can decide which treasures are the ones worth having. When you have spent your life, what will you want to have, or who will you want to have become, or what will you want to have given away, or what will you want to have left behind? What riches will seem enduring to you? What treasures could you possess that no one could take away from you?

IV

JAMES W. JONES' recent book, *In the Middle of This Road We Call Our Life,* has the provocative subtitle *The Courage to Search for Something More.* But, if we wanted to search for something more—if we wanted to discover what would make the spending of our life worthwhile—where would we look for it? Jones responds to this question by telling a story from India about an argument the gods had over where to hide the secret of life so that human beings would not find it.

"Bury it under a mountain," one god suggested, "they'll never find it there."

"No," others argued, "one day they will find a way to dig up mountains and then they will find it."

"Put it at the bottom of the deepest ocean," another god suggested.

"No," said the others, "someday humans will find a way to travel to the depths of the oceans and they will find it."

"Put it inside them," another god said, "men and women will not think of looking for it there."

All the gods agreed, the legend says, and hid the secret of life—the eternal treasure—within us.

V

THERE IS A HEAVENLY treasure worth pursuing in life—a treasure that would make the spending of your life worth it. But only you can decide what that treasure is. I cannot decide for you. The Apostle Paul cannot decide for you. Even Jesus cannot decide for you. When you have spent all the life given you, what will you want to have received in return, or whom will you want to have become, or what will you want to have left behind, or what will you want to have given away and to whom? What would make the spending of your life worth it?

When you have answered that you can go on to ask, "To what extent am I spending my life on the treasures that I believe are most worth having?" And finally, "How might I alter my life now, so that in the end I will be happy and grateful about the way I spent it?"

To come to the end of our life, grateful for the way we spent our life is to possess riches that no one can take away from us—it is to have gathered treasure that is truly worth having. Heavenly riches are riches that do not fade in the light of eternity. Heavenly riches are riches that we are delighted to have, even though they cost our life.

August 1995

Drainage Ditches for Jesus

◆   ◆   ◆

Beloved, we are God's children now . . .

— 1 John 3:2

WITH TWENTY OTHERS from St. Mark's—sixteen youth and four adults—I spent last week in rural Kentucky, repairing homes as part of the Appalachian Service Project. Thirty additional volunteers from Wisconsin and Minnesota were working on other homes in the same mountains around Chavies. Last week our three St. Mark's work teams put a new roof on a house, installed insulation, hung rain gutters, removed fireplaces, built steps, painted rooms, shoveled gravel, repaired a cistern and dug drainage ditches. My speciality was digging drainage ditches. We also washed dishes, swept floors, cleaned bathrooms and performed many of the other tasks that it takes to keep a group of fifty volunteers, eight staff, one child and three dogs going. Alongside the hard work there was frequent singing, much laughter, prayer, and, on the final evening, some tears.

I hadn't planned to talk about our work project this morning, but the youth in my work team kept bugging me about it. "Are you going to preach about this trip next Sunday," they asked. "No," I said, "I've already announced another topic and I've started working on it." "How can you be here all week and not talk about it?," they asked. "Easy," I said. But they persisted. On Friday, I asked, "Just what is it you want me to preach about on Sunday—digging drainage ditches for Jesus?" "Exactly!" they said. So I will talk about our week in Appalachia. Not what it meant to the youth, but what it meant to me.

The biblical text that underlies my thinking is part of a verse from the First Letter of John:

> Beloved, we are God's children now;
> it does not yet appear what we shall be,
> but we know that when he appears we shall
> be like him . . .
> — 1 John 3:2

As individual Christians, it is important that we recognize life lived in harmony with God's will whenever we get a glimpse of it. Otherwise, we will not understand the goal of our life—we will not understand where we are heading, much less what we might do to get there. We need those moments in life when we get a glimpse of where we are heading.

In recent years, we have heard references to Near Death Experiences, in which certain people came so close to death—indeed, it seemed to them that they had virtually died—that they received a new understanding of life. I've heard such people say that in the midst of this experience they understood for themselves what the purpose of life is—understood where they are meant to be going. I have never had a Near Death Experience, but every now and then I have a Near Life Experience—that is, every now and then I get so close to life as God intends it that I finally understand where it is that I'm supposed to be going. I had a Near Life Experience in Perry County, Kentucky, last week. I saw for myself some of the things that I believe God intends us to see.

II

FOR STARTERS, I saw that the walls or barriers which separate life from life can be transcended. Not only can Jesus Christ do this, but we can do this.

One day for morning devotions, a woman from the Minnesota group reminded us of the Bible passage in which Jesus says to the faithful who are gathered at his right hand: "I was hungry and you gave me food; I was thirsty and you gave me drink; I was naked and you clothed me; I was sick and you visited me; I was in prison and you came to me." The faithful were incredulous, asking, "When did we see you and do these things for you?" And Jesus answered, "Inasmuch as you did these things for people who needed them, you did them to me."

Jesus was nourished whenever a hungry person was fed and was refreshed whenever a thirsty person was given a drink because he had enlarged his self to include any who were in need. Jesus cared about others as though they were his own self.

We do this, too. You do this. There are people you care about as much as you care about yourself. Your child, perhaps; or a parent; or your spouse; or a special friend. If you had a son who was lost and hungry and a stranger gave him food, would not the stranger's gift to him also be a gift to you? If a special friend was sick and alone in a distant city and someone visited her, would that not also be a gift to you?

Several years ago a friend asked me to leave Indianapolis early one morning; fly to Lincoln, Nebraska; drive an hour to an outlying prison; visit for an hour with his son who was in solitary confinement because other prisoners had threatened his life; and then return home late that night. I did not know the son, but I went gladly because I cared about the father. At times we are so spiritually connected that to visit the son is to care about the father. When my son graduated from college two years ago and was looking for work in his chosen field, one of you spent time talking with him and helping him. Because you helped him, you cared for me. Surely, we all understand this.

In normal experience, we so extend ourselves spiritually to include a select few. Everyone does. But there need not be any limits on this. We can include many more others than we usually do. Spending time in the presence of Jesus expands our capacity to do this.

I saw several examples of this on our work trip last week. One of the most vivid concerned a twenty-year-old volunteer named Ralph and an eight-year-old boy whom we can here call Bobby. They met at the worksite where Ralph was assigned and the rapport between them was immediate. Before long Bobby was saying to Ralph, "It's like you're my older brother, man." When work ended each afternoon, Bobby asked Ralph if he would be back in the morning, and for four days Ralph was able to say Yes. On Friday Ralph had to say No, and Bobby gave him a small gift that he had made. In the evening Ralph told us about Bobby and cried because of Bobby's pain. Do you understand that in the future anyone who chooses to act like a brother to Bobby will be making a special gift to Ralph? Ralph has become like Christ in this instance. We can all become more Christlike in this way—by opening our hearts and increasing the number of persons for whom we care as we do about our own self. Spending time with Jesus increases our capacity to do this.

> Beloved, we are God's children now;
> it does not yet appear what we shall be,
> but we know that when he appears we shall
> be like him . . .

III

I ALSO SAW that love does not have to be felt to be practiced. To be spiritual is to practice love more often than we feel it.

Often we mistakenly think of love as being primarily a feeling. Jesus pushed us to consider what was going on inside us when we did good, but this does not mean we should care for people only when we feel like it. I prefer to think of love as an attitude with which we approach people and as actions which we offer people.

In the Appalachian Service Project, sometimes a close relationship with the family on whose home you are working springs up quickly and sometimes it doesn't; sometimes their need is apparent and you can see right away why you are there, and sometimes the need isn't as apparent; sometimes the work that needs doing fits the skills you already have and your mood at the moment and sometimes it doesn't. The truth is that there's a lot of work in life that nobody is just itching to do. One of our teams was assigned the task of installing insulation in a crawl space. The crawl space was hot, dirty, wet, cramped, and a breeding ground for critters. Who wanted to go in there? I'm not sure any one did. But people went. They girded their loins, as the Bible would say. They gritted their teeth and did it. Some distinguished themselves by really getting into it.

There were times on our work crew when the enthusiasm was lagging. You could tell by the faces that no one was particularly keen on hauling another bucket of heavy gravel up the hill, but they did it. Love can be an attitude and it can be actions—love can be a commitment—even when it isn't a feeling. Love can be a practice as in "Practice, practice, practice." When we practice love it sometimes turns into feeling. It is not the feeling that matters, but the practice.

That's what was going on in the Garden of Gethsemane when Jesus prayed, "Father, if it be possible let this cup pass from me" on the night before his crucifixion. Jesus could have escaped into the desert by scampering the few hundred yards that would have carried him over the rim of Mount Olivet. Instead, through prayer Jesus came to understand that what was facing him was his own cup. His to drink. He saw that it couldn't be passed, so he drank it.

This week when I saw youth giving themselves at times when they didn't feel like it, I was reminded that love which is practiced even when it is not spontaneously felt is very near to the Kingdom of God and to Christlikeness.

> Beloved, we are God's children now;
> it does not yet appear what we shall be,
> but we know that when he appears we shall
>   be like him . . .

IV

I ALSO SAW very clearly that the purpose of life is to give. The purpose of life is to make a contribution.

One of the besetting sins with which I have been struggling for years is grandiosity. I want to do things that will change everything. I want to do something big. But BIG isn't necessarily what is needed in God's Kingdom.

For Jesus, the way to bring in God's Kingdom was to plant a small seed. He not only talked like that, but he also lived like that. Most of his ministry was spent in the smallest and most humble villages of Galilee. He didn't even go to the ten major villages in the region. Toward the end of his ministry, he spent a few days in Jerusalem, but his major method of working was that of planting small seeds in humble regions.

That's how I came to see the work that our youth were doing last week. They weren't changing the whole world, they were lending a hand, they were expressing a little love, they were planting a seed. Perhaps that's all that's possible in this world—planting and tending seeds.

That became especially clear to me on Friday afternoon. Our primary task had been completed, so we hauled some gravel to a new site where work by another team will begin tomorrow morning. While we were there we were asked to dig the first length of another drainage ditch, no more than twenty-five feet. That segment will connect with other ditches soon to be dug. We didn't get to lay the plastic pipe or cover it with gravel, which is the fun part. We just dug the ditch and prepared it for the next step. As we shoveled and swung a pick axe, it was clear to me that we weren't doing away with hardship in Appalachia. We were digging the first segment of one ditch. But when we finished our work and were putting the tools away, my heart was strangely warmed because when I looked back I could see that the drainage ditch, which we had carved out of the red clay together, was a mighty fine ditch.

And then I saw for myself what Jesus kept trying to say in so many ways. That the purpose of our life is not to equate ourselves with God or to sit on our couch until we can do something magnificent and big. The purpose of our life is to serve. The purpose of our life is to do whatever needs doing. The purpose of our life is to make a contribution.

June 1995

Don't Let Your Death Stop You

◆ ◆ ◆

I consider that the sufferings of this present
time are not worth comparing to the glory that
is to be revealed to us.
— Romans 8:18

J
ESUS WAS KILLED and hastily entombed on a Friday afternoon. The women who had followed Jesus on foot from
Galilee to Jerusalem continued to follow him after his
death. When Joseph of Arimathea returned from Pontius Pilate,
where he had asked permission to bury the body of Jesus, the
women watched Joseph pry Jesus' body from the cross, lower
his body to the ground, wrap it in a linen cloth, and carry it to
a nearby tomb. Knowing, then, where Jesus' body had been
laid, the women returned to their quarters and prepared burial
ointments and embalming spices in the late afternoon hours
before the Jewish Sabbath descended. Luke says that on the
Sabbath day itself the women rested, in accordance with the
law. Then at first light on Sunday morning the women went
back to the tomb. They stepped inside the tomb but did not
see Jesus' body. While they were wondering what this might
mean, "two men in dazzling clothes" stood beside them and
asked "Why do you look for the living among the dead?" The
two men continued, "He is not here, but has risen." In one way,
shape, or form, Jesus had moved on, just as he had said he would.

I don't mean to suggest that the body of Jesus was still in
the tomb, but I do want to suggest that even if his body had
still been there, the statement "He is not here" would have
been an appropriate statement, and the question "Why do you
look for the living among the dead?" would have been appro-

priate, too. I am speaking from my own experience now and from the experience of others I have personally known. During thirty-five years of pastoral ministry I have never once stood beside the body of a person who has died and found myself saying, "I see that he is still here but dead" or "I see that she is still here but dead." Nor have I ever once heard a bereaved loved one stand beside a deathbed and say, "I see that he is still here but dead" or "I see that she is still here but dead." Not once have I heard that said. What I have myself felt each time—and what I have heard loved ones say—is something very close to what Luke reports that the "men in dazzling clothes" said to the women from Galilee: "He has gone." Or, "She has left us." Or, "He is no longer here." One has an overwhelming sense of that, when standing beside a deathbed, as you may well know. If you don't know now, one day you will know. It was not just the women inside Jesus' tomb who suddenly realized that they had gone to the wrong place. Any persons who stand beside the corpse of their beloved will very soon know that they are standing in the wrong place, that they are surrounded by an absence and can only wonder where their loved one has gone. "Why do you seek the living among the dead? He is not here," said the two men in dazzling clothes. The dead are not dead, the Bible is trying to tell us. Nor are they here. When you and I die, we will not be here nor will we be dead. Oh, much will come to an end at the time, for dying is serious business, but we will not be dead. Instead, as Paul said, "We will, in a twinkling, be changed." We do not yet know how we will be changed, but we will be changed and when we die we will not be dead. My hunch is that initially we will be amazed and that we will be traveling. You and I could not stop at death, even if we wanted to. When you hear the trumpet sound or the angels sing, hang onto your hat because that's traveling music. Death cannot stop us when we die. The only time that death can stop us is while we are still living on earth.

II

IN THE BIBLE, Jesus is portrayed as a man who could not be stopped by death—either before or after his dying.

For example, in the final weeks of his life, Jesus was able to set his face toward Jerusalem—he was able to go there to complete his work—even though he expected that by going to Jerusalem it was likely that he would suffer and die. He did not want to die. When we see Jesus praying in the Garden of Gethemane, we know that he did not want to die. But Jesus was a man whose reluctance to die did not prevent him from doing what he believed he was called by God to do. Death (or shall we say the fear of death) was not able to stop him. Jesus was able to risk himself in order to do what he believed was most important for him to do.

A similar example occurs when Jesus was on trial before Pontius Pilate. Pilate was trying to force Jesus to knuckle under to his worldly power. Pilate tried to intimidate Jesus by threatening to use force against him. But Jesus did not knuckle under—Jesus did not yield—either to Pilate or to the threat of death. Instead, he said to the Roman governor, "You have no power over me." That is another way of saying, "You cannot really kill me—you cannot ultimately destroy me—besides taking away my earthly life, what could you possibly do to me?" Every person of faith can receive from God the courage and the power to stand erect in that way. There is no way that we can secure our life, but we can as Jesus said "let go of our life." As the old hymn says, we can "stand on God's promises." When we do stand on God's promises—when we say to the world, "I am going to do what God wants, because there is nothing besides taking away my life that you can do to me," we become strangely powerful and remarkably free.

III

THERE IS ANOTHER way that death can stop us before we die. Because all people eventually die, we may choose to protect ourselves by not loving another human being too deeply. We can make a bargain with death that goes something like this: "I will choose not to love deeply, so that I will not have to painfully grieve." If we are not able or willing to love, because we are afraid to grieve, death is already having its way with us.

I have long been interested in the story of Lazarus' death, which is recorded in John's Gospel. Lazarus, you may remember, was a close friend of Jesus. When Jesus went to the city where Lazarus was sick, he discovered that Lazarus had already died. When Jesus was taken to Lazarus' tomb, Jesus experienced grief. The Bible says succinctly, "Jesus wept." That is, even Jesus grieved. If we care deeply for any other person, one way or another at some time or another, we will painfully grieve. If we do not care for others, because we are afraid to grieve, death is already having its way with us.

In the Sermon on the Mount, Jesus said to his disciples, "Blessed are those who mourn, for they shall be comforted." This is a way of saying that ultimately to love deeply and then painfully grieve is far, far better than to have never loved or grieved. After we have died, we will all understand this. The time is coming, Paul said, when the sting of death—that is, the pain of grief—will be taken away. But the removal of this pain will not occur until we are beyond this life. When we are no longer mortal, but are ourselves immortal, we will be happy that we have both loved and grieved. To both love and mourn is to come very close to the heart of God. To both love and mourn is to come very close to understanding what the meaning of life is.

Death cannot stop us when we die. When we die, people will plainly see and say that we are gone. "He is not here" and "She is gone," they will say of us. We will be moving on, no matter what. It is only while we are living on earth that death can stop us, by frightening us or by discouraging us.

IV

RECENTLY I READ the book *Life Work* by Donald Hall. Donald Hall is a former professor of English at the University of Michigan who gave up his position, tenure, and guaranteed income some twenty years ago in order to move with his wife to an old family farmhouse in New Hampshire, from which he makes his living as a writer. He is a poet, a short story writer, a novelist, an essayist, and a writer of children's books and literary reviews.

His book *Life Work* is a bit of a journal, in that he chose to write a little each morning before moving on to other projects. The first morning on which he wrote happened to be on the anniversary of the death of his good friend and pastor who had died exactly two years before. In fact, Don Hall was sitting with his pastor in the early morning hours—holding his hand— until shortly before he died. As so often seems to happen, it was in the brief moment that Don Hall left the bedside to get a cup of coffee that his friend Jack died. In the opening pages of this book he talks about his love for Jack and his grief at his passing.

By the time the book was completed just three months later, Don Hall was no longer talking about Jack's cancer, but his own. Already two-thirds of his liver had been cut out of him. Chemotherapy would begin the next day. No one could tell him that the chemo would help, only that it might. What he could be sure of was that his appetite and energy would diminish and that they would be replaced by nausea. He was not in immediate danger at book's end, but he was unclear as to what the future had in store. "What," he asks, "shall I do?" He could, of course, quit. Give in completely to his disease. Or he could deny. He could pretend that nothing had changed. Instead, he closed the journal like this:

If little poems announce themselves I will open the door. But I will undertake no more long projects. I will do short stories, children's books, new short poems, maybe another essay of this length—but no more long-term projects. Today if I begin a thought about 1995 I do not finish the thought. It is easier, and it remains pleasant, to undertake short endeavors which absorb me as much as any work can. There is only one long-term project.

I admired that. It seemed to me a faithful way to meet his situation. No doubt there are other faithful ways. Starting a thirty-volume encyclopedia might be a faithful way, just so you knew what you were doing. Donald Hall is being faithful in that he is now taking the possibility of his own death into account, as we would all be wise to take the possibility of our own death into account. Donald Hall will not pretend; nor will he deny. For now, there will be no long-term writing projects. On the other hand, he will not let death stop him. He will continue going forward—just as Jesus did when walking to Jerusalem—doing what work he still can and loving his wife and his friends day by day.

Then Donald Hall closes with that intriguing final line: "There is only one long-term project." That's provocative. As we live, there is only one long-term project. What could that project be? That seems similar to what Jesus said to Martha, the sister of Lazarus—that in the midst of all our busyness, there is only one thing needful. What is the one thing needful? If it is true that we are eternal—if it is true that we couldn't stop at death, even if we wanted to—if we are moving on no matter what—if, as Paul says, our lives are wrapped up in God far more than we can now see or know—what do you suppose that one important project is? It's good to work on that project now, Jesus would say. It's important that we not let death stop or frighten or discourage us.

April 1994

. . . Forever. Amen

◆　◆　◆

For thine is the kingdom, and the power, and
the glory, forever. Amen

— From the Lord's Prayer

THE WORDS ". . . FOREVER. Amen" are the last two words of
the Lord's Prayer as prayed by Protestant Christians.
These were not Jesus' words but were added by the early
church in the second century. When a friend learned that I had
been reflecting on the words ". . . forever. Amen," he said, "Oh,
I get it, on a clear day you can see forever." That wasn't what I
had been thinking at the time, but I can see a way in which he's
right. On a clear day—that is, on a day in which we are clear—
we probably can see all the way to forever. But I'd prefer to turn
that around and let the insight flow the other way: Whenever
we are seeing from forever, it becomes a clear day. I might even
go so far as to say that it is never a clear day until we are seeing
from forever.

II

IN THE BIBLE stories of Good Friday and the Saturday after Jesus'
death, because the disciples of Jesus are not seeing from the
standpoint of forever, for them it is not at all a clear day. They
are seeing all of life from the perspective of right now and,
therefore, the skies are darkened by their own pain, fears, grief,
tears, and disappointments. Not only has Jesus been taken
away from them, but he was quickly and easily disposed of as

an annoyance to Rome after first being mocked and humiliated. The purpose of the execution was not simply to eliminate Jesus, but was also to discredit Jesus. The intention was to get rid of Jesus morally as well as physically—to do away with his teaching, example and influence every bit as much as to get rid of his living, breathing flesh.

By killing its leader, Rome was trying to destroy the Jesus Movement itself, but on Easter morning that effort began to unravel. When Mary Magdalene went to the tomb where Jesus had been buried, even though it was still dark, she began to have a clear day. The Gospel of John says that Mary saw two angels sitting where the body of Jesus *had* lain. That's John way of telling us that Mary was beginning to see from forever. Luke tells of two disciples on the road to Emmaus meeting a stranger who helped them to see that Jesus' death did not mean that he had lost favor with God, but had scriptural precedence. In the face of this news, their "hearts burned within them," and they sensed that Jesus himself was near. That is Luke's way of telling us that the two disciples were beginning to see from forever. One-by-one the followers of Jesus were themselves resurrected as they dug themselves out of the darkness of right now and began to see life from the perspective of forever.

III

CHRISTIANITY HAS LONG taught that time and eternity—that is, "right now" and "forever"—exist side by side. It isn't that first we have "now" and much later we will have "forever." One of the mysteries of life is that time and eternity, right now and forever, exist side by side.

I like the way Phillips Brooks, a towering preacher in Boston a century ago, almost put it. In a sermon, "Standing Before God," he talked about how close eternity is to time, although he still had them laid end to end.

The life which we are living now is more aware than we know of the life that is to come. Death, which separates the two, is not, as it so often has been pictured, like a great thick wall. It is rather like a soft and yielding curtain, through which we cannot see, but which is always waving and trembling with the impulses that come out of the life which lies on the other side of it. We are never wholly unaware that the curtain is not the end of everything. Sounds come to us, muffled and dull, but still indubitably real, through its thick folds. Every time that a new soul passes through that veil from mortality to immortality . . . it almost seems as if the curtain is going to open to give us a sight of the unseen things beyond it; and although we are forever disappointed, the shadowy expectation always comes back to us again, when we see the curtain stirred by another friend's departure. After our friend has passed, we can almost see the curtain, which he stirred, moving, tremulously for a while, before it settles once more into stillness.

Time and eternity, mortality and immortality, right now and forever are not separated by a thick, impenetrable wall, but by a soft, yielding curtain. That curtain, however, is not at the end of the hallway. As you yourself may already have sensed, eternity, immortality, and forever are right beside us. If you sit quietly for even a few moments sometime today, you will hear familiar voices whispering to you from the other side of that curtain. Eternity is not at the end of the hallway. Eternity is all around us. We begin to see clearly when we look at now from the standpoint of forever.

IV

ANOTHER WAY TO talk about "forever" is to talk about it as "God's point of view." "Forever" isn't later, "forever" is now. "Forever" is always. "Forever" is life when seen from God's point of view. It is not so much that on a clear day we can see forever. It's more like our clear days are the one's in which we are looking

at life from God's point of view. That, by the way, is who Jesus
Christ is. Jesus Christ is human life lived from forever. Jesus
Christ is human life lived from God's point of view.

V

PHILLIPS BROOKS TALKED about muffled voices coming from the
other side of the curtain and of the curtain itself moving and
trembling, but those are not the only ways that the eternal
makes itself known in time. It is also true that the eternal
occasionally crashes into time, dramatically changing the way
we are seeing whatever is going on in time. This is very hard to
talk about, although we have all experienced it.

What I mean by the eternal crashing into time are those
moments in which our normal consciousness is altered, and
we are suddenly seeing life from God's point of view. It isn't
that we are still saying, "I ought to be seeing life from God's
point of view," but that suddenly and unexpectedly we are
seeing life from God's point of view. We have all had moments
like this, but let me try to point to the kind of moment I'm
talking about by using a biblical example.

Consider Peter on the night Jesus was arrested. Jesus had
predicted that Peter would deny him before morning, but Peter
who was still living in the obscurity of time said, "No, I'll never
do that." Later, when Peter senses himself in danger, he does
exactly what he said he would not do. Outside a house where
Jesus is being questioned, a woman says of Peter, "I know him;
I've seen him before; this is one of Jesus' followers!" Peter,
concerned for saving his own skin—that is, caring more about
time than about eternity—says, "No, I'm not a follower of
Jesus. I never even knew him."

Just then two things happen. First. Peter hears a rooster
beginning to crow. If you can imagine the pause that is suddenly beginning to insert itself into Peter's time—if you can

imagine the momentary confusion that Peter begins to feel when the cock starts to crow—if you have a sense of what that is like when Peter begins to pause and his brain starts rapidly scanning his memory because he has the feeling that he has forgotten something—that break in his rhythm—that unexpected flash of bewilderment—is what it feels like when what we call the eternal, or God's point of view, is about to come crashing in. And then, even while Peter is groping for whatever it is he has forgotten, he looks up and there is Jesus. Jesus has seen and heard everything! And in the split second when their eyes meet, everything changes for Peter because now he sees himself through the eyes of Jesus Christ. Now he sees himself from God's perspective. Saving his skin—that is, "time"—no longer matters to Peter. Now only God's point of view matters to Peter. His concerns for time have been swept away, because the eternal—that which is truly important—has come crashing in. Time stands still. It is as though we are frozen in time when the eternal comes crashing in. You have been caught like that—you have been frozen like that—haven't you, because you had been living in the obliviousness of time and suddenly the eternal came crashing in? It is important that you search your own life for those moments in which everything looked different because the eternal came crashing in.

VI

SOMETIMES IN A motion picture—usually in a mystery, or a spy story, or some other suspense film—as the action is flowing along you will suddenly hear the click of a still camera's shutter and then the action will be momentarily frozen—and then the flow starts up again and then the frame is frozen again—and the scene always looks different when the action is frozen— new and deeper meanings always arise when the action is frozen. You also notice that more is going on than you realized.

What is happening is changed by this new perspective. Whenever in your life, you feel frames of action being frozen, that is when the eternal—God's point of view—is breaking in.

A few years ago, one night here at church a woman collapsed after a Bible study. An ambulance was called. She had had a seizure of some kind. By the time I learned of it, the ambulance was pulling away. I hurried to my car and followed the ambulance. The lights were on inside the ambulance, and I could see another of our members bent over the woman who had collapsed. And as I was driving along behind, watching the action, the kind of click that I'm trying to talk about occurred. The action was frozen. Suddenly I was seeing the woman who was helping, not through my eyes, but through Christ's eyes. Through Christ's eyes, I saw how gentle she was; how merciful she was; how present she was; how spiritual she was. And therefore I saw how elevated she was–how elevated she was and will always be in God's eyes. That changed perspective is what I mean by the eternal breaking in.

VII

THE DAY WE CALL Easter is a wonderful day because on that day and on the days afterward, various followers of Jesus, experienced forever breaking in. When that happened it wasn't that they tried to see Jesus differently. They did see Jesus differently.

No longer did they see Jesus through Rome's eyes, or through death's eyes, or even through their own eyes. Instead, they were mysteriously able to see Jesus through God's eyes. They saw not only how kind Jesus had been, how humble he had been, how forgiving he had been, how peaceful he had been, how loving he had been, but they also saw how alive he was and how elevated he was, because they were able to see him from the standpoint of forever—because they were able to see him through God's eyes. When they saw Jesus through God's eyes, their pain and disappointment disappeared and were replaced with rejoicing.

Our pain and disappointment disappear, too, when we are seeing life from the standpoint of forever. It isn't so much that on a clear day we can see forever, but that when we are seeing from forever, it becomes a clear day. I might go so far as to say that it is never a clear day until we are seeing from forever.

April 1995